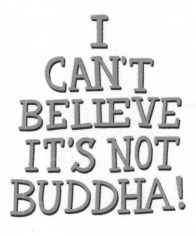

I CAN'T BELIEVE IT'S NOT BUDDHA!

I CAN'T BELIEVE IT'S NOT BUDDHA!

WHAT FAKE BUDDHA QUOTES CAN TEACH US ABOUT BUDDHISM

BODHIPAKSA

PARALLAX
PRESS

PARALLAX.ORG

Parallax Press
P.O. Box 7355
Berkeley, California 94707
parallax.org

Parallax Press is the publishing division of Plum Village
Community of Engaged Buddhism, Inc.

Cover illustration © Kayla Stark
Cover and text design by John Barnett | 4eyesdesign.com
Author photo © Joseph Perna Photography

ISBN: 978-1-946764-35-5

Library of Congress Cataloging-in-Publication Data
Names: Bodhipaksa, 1961- author.
Title: I can't believe it's not Buddha! : fake Buddha quotes and
   what they can teach us about Buddhism / Bodhipaksa.
Description: Berkeley, CA : Parallax Press, 2018. | Includes
   bibliographical references.
Identifiers: LCCN 2018011261 (print) | LCCN 2018018425
   ebook) | ISBN 9781946764362 (ebook) | ISBN 9781946764355
   (paperback)
Subjects: LCSH: Buddhism--Anecdotes. | Gautama Buddha--
   Miscellanea. | Common fallacies. | BISAC: RELIGION /
   Buddhism / Zen (see also PHILOSOPHY / Zen).
   | REFERENCE / Quotations. | HUMOR / Form / Anecdotes.
Classification: LCC BQ4060 (ebook) | LCC BQ4060 .B63 2018
   (print) | DDC 294.3--dc23
LC record available at https://lccn.loc.gov/2018011261

1 2 3 4 5 / 22 21 20 19 18

To my children, Maia and Malkias, for teaching me patience and making me a better human being.

The highest compliment you can pay
an author is to misquote him.

—*Ethel Fischbaum*

CONTENTS

● ●

INTRODUCTION

The Buddha is one of the world's most misquoted people. Sayings that claim to be by him, but aren't, abound in Facebook memes, quote sites, blog articles, and even in published books. I call them Fake Buddha Quotes—a quick and dirty term that's intended to be concise, playful, and just a little provocative.

How did I get started on this quest? A cartoon by Randall Munroe shows a figure sitting hunched in front of a computer screen. A voice off-panel asks, "Are you coming to bed?" The computer user replies, "I can't. This is important. Someone on the internet is wrong." Munroe and I have never met, but he has somehow gazed into the depths of my very soul.

Almost a decade ago, perplexed, bemused, and sometimes alarmed by the fact that the majority of "Buddha quotes" I saw on social media were things the Buddha never said, I began documenting the Fake Buddha Quote phenomenon. I cataloged them on a blog, identified their origins when I could, and offered some genuine scriptural quotations to show what the Buddha (as best we know) really taught. Fake quotes became teachable moments.

My suspicions about these spurious quotes may be aroused by a number of things. One common giveaway is the style, which may be too flowery, poetic, or literary. Another is the vocabulary, which is often much too contemporary to be the words of someone who lived some 2,500 years ago.

If someone told you that "Technological progress, and civilization generally, could be compared to an axe in the hand of a pathological criminal," was a quote from William Shakespeare, I hope you'd be suspicious. You'd probably think that the vocabulary was too modern, and assume that a sentence like that would be more at home in the twentieth or twenty-first centuries. (In fact it's something Albert Einstein wrote in 1917.) I'm pretty sure that no one has ever tried to pass off this particular quotation as being from Shakespeare, but I've seen plenty of "Buddha quotes" that are just as anachronistic.

The earliest scriptures are recorded in languages like Pali and Sanskrit, which have very different grammatical rules from English. This can give even the best translations a stilted and clunky feel. Knowing that one fact, here's a little test for you. Which of the following quotes about virtue do you think is more likely to come from India 2,500 years ago?

1. "The virtues, like the Muses, are always seen in groups. A good principle was never found solitary in any breast."
2. "For a person endowed with virtue, consummate in virtue, there is no need for an act of will, 'May freedom from remorse arise in me.' It is in the nature of things that freedom from remorse arises in a person endowed with virtue, consummate in virtue."

If you picked the second, you're well on the way to becoming a fully licensed Fake Buddha Quote–buster. Congratulations!

If the first quote sounds like something from the nineteenth century, that's because it is. Although it's often attributed to the Buddha, it's actually from an 1807 book by Jane Porter, a Scottish novelist, playwright, and literary figure. The reference to the Muses—Ancient Greek goddesses the Buddha would have had no familiarity with—is a dead giveaway.

The second quote is from a Buddhist discourse called the Cetana Sutta. Notice that "freedom from remorse" and "a person endowed with virtue, consummate in virtue" each appear twice in two short sentences. This is typical in a literature that was originally oral, where repetition helps with memorization. There's also some awkwardness about the abrupt way the embedded quote is dropped in, which happens because Pali treats direct speech very differently from English.

And how about these two quotes on the topic of attachment? Which do you think is a genuine quote from the Buddha?

1. "Don't be attached to my philosophy and doctrine. Attachment to any religion is simply another form of mental illness."
2. "From attachment springs grief, from attachment springs fear. For one who is

wholly free from attachment there is no grief, whence then fear?"

This one might be trickier, but if you thought the first quote was suspect because "mental illness" is a modern term, you'd be correct.* Some of us might *wish* that the first one was something the Buddha had said, and it's often been taken as such, but it's actually by a twentieth-century Tibetan Buddhist teacher. The genuine passage is unfortunately less quotable.

A subtler giveaway is when quotes clash with what the Buddha taught, although to know that you have to have some familiarity with the Buddhist scriptures. For example, the quote, "Doubt everything. Find your own light," might sound genuine unless you were aware that the Buddha didn't talk about doubt in a positive sense, but only as a state of confusion.

Sometimes, though, it's hard to tell whether or not a quote is legitimate. I've been convinced a particular saying is genuine only to discover that it's fake, and vice versa. Some fake quotes even fool Buddhist scholars, making their way

---

* The Buddha did contrast being "afflicted in body" (i.e physically sick) with being "afflicted in mind," but he didn't use the latter term in the same way we'd use the term "mentally ill."

into academic books and papers. This is understandable. When you've seen something quoted frequently by people you trust, you naturally assume it must be genuine.

So how do Fake Buddha Quotes arise?

First, there's the phenomenon of "quotation promotion": a tendency for quotes to be reassigned from relatively less well-known to more famous authors. Presumably this is because to many people a quote written by, say, Ethel Fischbaum (whom I just invented) sounds less authoritative than one attributed to Albert Einstein or Winston Churchill. You don't want to pass on an inspiring quote to your Facebook friends only to have half of them respond with "Who the heck's Ethel Fischbaum?" On the other hand those same friends might think well of you seeing you quote, and thereby associate yourself with, some literary or historical giant.

The "mental illness" quote is an example of another phenomenon we could call a "slip of the ear." This happens when a teacher paraphrases the Buddha's teaching while giving a talk ("The Buddha said that . . .") and then a transcriber or editor mistakes the paraphrase as an actual quote.

Then there are what I call "lost in translation" quotes. Sometimes, due to lack of skill or because the translator wants to insert his or her own beliefs—creating a "new, improved" version of the Buddha's teaching—translators distort the meaning of the original. Take, for example, the following pair of quotes:

1. "Clearly understanding one's own welfare, let one be intent upon the good."
2. "Your work is to discover your work and then with all your heart give yourself to it."

Would you believe these are both translations of the same verse? The first quote is a literal rendition, while the other seems to be composed of one percent actual translation and ninety-nine percent poetic inspiration. Unfortunately, the fake version from this example is quoted far more often than the legitimate one. After all, while the more literal translation doesn't exactly sizzle, the language of discovering your work and of giving yourself to it with all your heart sounds rather appealing.

Lastly, I'm convinced that sometimes people just make up a spiritual-sounding quote and stick "The Buddha" on the end. As we all know, there are plenty of trolls on the internet.

When I use the provocative term "fake," I'm saying nothing more than that a quote is misattributed—that we can't legitimately claim it was said by the Buddha. Whether it's in line with the

Buddha's teachings, inspiring, or personally meaningful to you are other matters entirely. So bear in
mind that if I debunk the *origins* of a quote that
you like, I'm not necessarily saying that it's not
useful or inspiring. (There are some Fake Buddha
Quotes that I really *wish* the Buddha had said.)

The extent to which these spurious quotations
have displaced the genuine article is striking.
There are many blog posts along the lines of
"Buddha Quotes That Will Change Your Life"
that are composed almost entirely of things that
the Buddha never said. In this age of self-pub-
lishing, you can even buy entire books composed
mainly of fake quotes. It seems that many people
are drawn more strongly to fake quotations than
to legitimate ones—presumably because the fakes
sound more literary and poetic.

In fact, the Buddha foresaw that his followers
would be tempted to ignore his own words:

> *They will listen when discourses that are*
> *literary works—the works of poets, elegant in*
> *sound, elegant in rhetoric, the work of outsid-*
> *ers, words of disciples—are recited. They will*
> *lend ear and set their hearts on knowing them.*

For the purposes of this book I've chosen
fifty quotes from the hundreds I've collected

over the years. You'll find all of them circulating on social media, in blog posts, or published in books. Many of them are even available on mugs, T-shirts, and fridge magnets.

As we examine these quotes, I'll point out what made me suspect their authenticity, identify where I can who the true authors were, and offer examples of legitimate quotes from the Buddhist scriptures. We'll examine these quotes in alphabetical order, giving us an A to Z of things the Buddha never said.

But before we begin, let me confess to fallibility. I've endeavored to be accurate in this book, but if I've slipped up, I beg your forgiveness. As Voltaire said, "We are all formed of frailty and error; let us reciprocally pardon each other's folly." Or as no one ever said, until now, "To err is human, to forgive is Buddha-ful."

THE QUOTES
• • • • • • • • • • •• •• • • •• • • • • • • ••

1. ˙All descriptions of reality are temporary hypotheses.˙

If you were to come unsuspectingly upon this quote, you might think, "Wow! That's so scientific! The Buddha was so ahead of his time!" Unfortunately, however, this quote sounds contemporary because it is. The earliest source that I've found for this is *From Science to God*, by Peter Russell, published in 2002. I don't know why Russell attributed it to the Buddha, or if he was the first to do so. I asked him where he got the quote from, and unfortunately even he can't remember.

The notion that descriptions of reality are merely temporary hypotheses might seem at first glance to be very much in line with the Buddha's teachings. He described reality as being "beyond the grasp of concepts," or *atakka-vacara*. The Buddha regarded even his own Dharma* as no more than a means to an end. He once described the teachings as being like a raft, which we can use to cross a river but which we have to abandon once we reach the other side.

> *Having got across and arrived at the other shore, the man thinks: "This raft, indeed, has been very helpful to me. Carried by it, and laboring with hands and feet, I got safely across to the other shore. Should I not pull it up now to the dry land or let it float in the water, and then go as I please?" By acting thus, monks, would that man do what should be done with a raft. In the same way, monks, have I shown to you the Teaching's similitude to a raft: as having the purpose of crossing over, not the purpose of being clung to.*

---

* *Dharma* is a Sanskrit word with a wide range of meaning, including Reality, teaching, moral law, principle, mental state, and phenomenon. In Pali, the language of the earliest scriptures, it's *Dhamma*. Here it means "teaching."

So from our point of view, his teachings are indeed to be taken as guides to be followed until we get to the point where we see Reality as he saw it. For us the teachings may be considered as hypotheses to be checked out in the light of our experience. For the Buddha, on the other hand, his teachings were not hypotheses. Hypotheses are speculations, while the Dharma was his attempt to express, in necessarily limited language, something that he'd seen directly.

When the Buddha says that we shouldn't cling to his teachings, he means that they're not meant to be *believed*, but to be acted upon. Believing in a raft has little benefit; the point is to use it to get across the water.

In short, this quote misrepresents how the Buddha regarded his own teachings, although it does remind us that *we* should treat the Buddha's teachings as instructions to be tested through practice, rather than propositions to be believed.

2. 'All things are perfect exactly as they are.'

Although you'll see statements similar to this quote in later Buddhist teachings (and especially in Zen Buddhism, which is where this one comes from), there's nothing to suggest that the Buddha himself thought that everything is perfect as it is. In fact, his emphasis tended to be on the fact that there are many things wrong in life.

You may be aware that one of the Buddha's key teachings is the Four Noble Truths. The first of these is that there is suffering (not that *life* is suffering, but just that there is suffering in life):*

> *Birth is suffering, aging is suffering, sickness is suffering, death is suffering, sorrow and lamentation, pain, grief and despair are suffering; association with the loathed is suffering, dissociation from the loved is suffering, not to get what one wants is suffering.*

Oy vey! Life is strangely generous in bestowing opportunities for both physical and emotional pain!

The quote in question can be spiritually useful or a hindrance, depending on how it's interpreted.

When something unpleasant has happened in our lives, such as a loss, it can be a great comfort

---

* In case you're wondering, the other three noble truths are: that suffering has a cause, which is grasping; that there is a state of freedom from suffering, which is Nirvana; and that freedom from suffering can be attained by following the Eightfold Path.

to accept that things can't be otherwise than they are at the moment. The alternative, which is to rail at how things are, is what the Buddha described as sorrow, lamentation, grief, and despair. These reactions just add to our suffering. (See also #34.) As the Buddha didn't say, "Pain is inevitable. Suffering is optional."

And yet things are obviously not perfect. There is suffering in the world. There is war, famine, and poverty. There is loneliness, addiction, and cruelty. The Buddha in no way encouraged us to ignore these things, and in fact he encouraged us to act with compassion toward those who are suffering. We don't want to accept the unacceptable.

In summary: this is a useful quote when we apply it to our own suffering. Applying it to others' suffering—not so much.

The viewpoint that all things are perfect is found in Western philosophy, too. Thomas Aquinas, in his *Summa Theologica,* says, "Existence is the most perfect of all things," and the seventeenth-century Dutch philosopher Baruch Spinoza said in his *Ethics,* "Reality and perfection I understand to be one and the same thing." As we'll see again, Fake Buddha Quotes spread more easily when they resonate with preexisting ideas.

3. 'All worldlings are mad.'

This particular quote has fooled even scholars of Buddhism. It is found in any number of books, magazines, and academic journals, to the extent that I was surprised to discover that it doesn't come from the Buddha.

This saying actually comes from commentaries on the Buddhist scriptures, and not from the scriptures themselves. For example, Buddhaghosa's fifth-century *Path of Purification (Visuddhimagga)* says, "The worldling is like a madman." The term "worldling" (*puthujjana*) refers to an ordinary, unenlightened person. If you're not awakened, you're a *puthujjana*.

You might notice that Buddhaghosa doesn't say the worldling *is* mad, just that the worldling is *like* a mad person. Buddhaghosa explains that what he means is simply that, like insane people, we act without considering the consequences of our actions.

Although the Buddha didn't say that we're mad, he did point out that we're under the sway of four cognitive distortions, namely: believing that impermanent things are permanent; believing that sources of suffering are sources of pleasure; believing that things that aren't intrinsic to us are ourselves; and believing that things that are wholesome are unwholesome.

Until we're awakened, we don't see things as they really are, and so many of the things we do to find happiness actually cause us stress and conflict. Seeing the world in such a skewed way is certainly delusional, and sometimes may seem a bit crazy. But the Buddha didn't say we're off our rockers.

Occasionally this quote is preceded by the words, "Human stupidity is boundless." That part's fake too.

4. 'Ambition is like love, impatient both of delays and rivals.'

If you're familiar with the early scriptures, you'll probably realize that this quote is too literary and *bon mot*-ish to be something the Buddha said. In fact, it's from a 1641 play, *The Sophy*, by the Anglo-Irish poet and courtier, Sir John Denham.

Denham is saying that ambition and love are similar in that they make us—confused worldlings as we are—rash and jealous. In many ways the Buddha too saw worldly ambition as a negative thing:

[Thinking] "Let both laymen and monks
think that it was done by me. In every work,
great and small, let them follow me"—such
is the ambition of the fool; thus his desire and
pride increase.

However, his last words to his disciples were "strive diligently," so he wasn't exactly encouraging us to be slackers, or to practice the sort of "acceptance" some people talk about where they say we're not supposed to want to change.

And in a more material sense, he encouraged his householder followers (that is, those who weren't monks and nuns but had families and jobs) to work hard and to create wealth:

Heedful at administering
or working at one's occupation,
maintaining one's life in tune,
one protects one's store of wealth.

The important thing, however, was that they were to practice nonattachment to their wealth by using it to help others. So the Buddha was against selfish ambition, but in favor of ambition aimed at spiritual goals, such as improving ourselves or the world.

5. "An idea that is developed and put into action is more important than an idea that exists only as an idea."

This quote is very Buddhist in spirit, but in tone it's unlike anything I've come across in the scriptures. It's actually from the book *Serious Creativity* by the Maltese physician and psychologist Edward de Bono.

Exactly how this was taken to be a quote from the Buddha is a mystery. Maybe someone who read the quote didn't know who de Bono was (he's best known for having coined the term "lateral thinking," incidentally) and thought it would sound more authoritative with the Buddha's name attached to it. This is what I've called "quotation promotion."

There's not much to quibble about with the quote itself. The closest parallel in the Buddhist scriptures I know of is found in verse 19 of the Dhammapada:

> *Much though he recites the sacred texts, but acts not accordingly, that heedless man is like a cowherd who only counts the cows of others—he does not partake of the blessings of the holy life.*

The Buddha is saying that memorizing, reciting, and studying the instructions for building the raft is pointless (see #1). A raft has the purpose of crossing over, so build your raft and then use it!

One of the problems with many of the quotes that fill our Facebook feeds is that we may think they're inspiring, but we move on to the next quote, status update, or cute cat photo before we have a chance to act on them. They remain mere ideas because we don't take the time to put them into action.

6. 'As rain falls equally on the just and unjust, do not burden your heart with judgments but rain your kindness equally upon all.'

The first part of this quote is adapted from Matthew 5:45, which says, "For He maketh His sun to rise on the evil and on the good, and sendeth rain on the just and on the unjust."

The second part probably derives from an actual Buddhist scripture, the Lotus Sutra. An extensive passage from that work depicts the Buddha comparing himself to a great rain cloud, nourishing the world. The part about not judging is (somewhat condensed) as follows:

...the Buddha
Appears here in the World,
Like unto a great cloud
Universally covering all things ...
Upon all I ever look
Everywhere impartially,
Without distinction of persons ...
Ever to all beings
I preach the Law equally;
As I preach to one person,
So I preach to all.

Now this is where I risk upsetting some Buddhists. Although the Lotus Sutra purports to be a teaching from the historical Buddha, and is revered in East Asia as his highest teaching, it was actually composed hundreds of years after his death. It's without doubt a work of great spiritual profundity: but there's no chance that it was taught by the historical Buddha.

For the Buddha, compassion was certainly to be extended without judging whether a person "deserved" it or not, but there was also a need to judge whether people's actions were right or wrong. Judging was not to be avoided, but instead to be done wisely:

He who does not judge others arbitrarily, but passes judgment impartially according to the truth, that sagacious man is a guardian of law and is called just.

Oh, and judging should be done without hatred or anger, too.

Anyway, my favorite teaching on rain and impartiality is the following, often said to be by the English judge Charles Bowen:

The rain it raineth on the just.
And also on the unjust fella:
But chiefly on the just, because,
The unjust steals the just's umbrella.

I've found no evidence that Bowen actually said this, however.

7. *'Awake. Be the witness of your thoughts. You are what observes, not what you observe.'*

This quote, which is actually two quotes cobbled together, is a sneaky one.

The first part, "Awake. Be the witness of your

thoughts," comes from Thomas Byrom's version of the Dhammapada (verse 327, to be specific), which is of course part of the Buddhist scriptures. However, Byrom's Dhammapada is not so much a translation as it is a work of original poetry.

The relevant part of Dhammapada verse 327 could be translated very literally as "Be devoted to heedfulness. Guard your mind." Now, "Be devoted to heedfulness" is much more specific than the command to "awake." Heedfulness is a technical term for a vigilant state of mindfulness called *appamada*. The word "Awake," on the other hand, naturally suggests *bodhi*, or enlightenment, which is not what this verse is talking about.

Also, "be the witness of your thoughts" is way off. The Dhammapada asks us to "guard the mind" (*citta*), rather than to witness thoughts. The word "mind" includes much more than just thoughts. It includes intentions, habits, and emotions.

Byrom's word choices are especially misleading when they're seen in the context of the second part of the quote. "You are what observes, not what you observe" is from Robert Earl Burton's 1995 book, *Self-Remembering*. Both the Byrom and the Burton parts of the quote seem to be based on the Hindu teaching of a "witnessing consciousness," which, according to that tradition, is our "true self" or *atman*. According to this teaching you are not your feelings, thoughts, body, or other experiences. You are instead that which is aware of those things. This might seem perfectly reasonable to many modern readers, but it's not what the Buddha taught.

While the Hindu tradition teaches that we need to realize the *atman*, or true Self, the Buddhist tradition teaches that we should realize the opposite: *anatman*, or the absence of a true Self. Although the Buddha agreed that you're not your feelings, thoughts, body, or other experiences, he also stated that neither are you your awareness of those things.

Now you might wonder what this leaves as being "you" or "yourself," and in fact the very point of the Buddha's teaching is that we shouldn't identify anything whatsoever as being ourselves. While it's common to hear that the Buddha taught a doctrine that there was no self, what *anatta* actually means is "not self." He encouraged us to observe the body, feelings, and even our consciousness with the awareness "This is not me. This is not mine. This is *not myself*." The aim is to live free from defining our selves in any way.

Byrom (see also #28, #45) was in fact a practicing Hindu, while Burton described himself as a teacher of the "Fourth Way," which amalgamated concepts from esoteric Christianity, Buddhism, and Hinduism. This is one of these cases where a nice-sounding and popular quote attributed to the Buddha manages to distort and even subvert his teaching.

8. ˙Believe nothing, no matter where you read it, or who said it, no matter if I have said it, unless it agrees with your own reason and your own common sense.˙

Here again we have a Buddhist scripture that's rendered in such a fashion that it ends up saying the opposite of what the Buddha taught. The Kalama Sutta, the scripture this purports to be from, actually says that reason and common sense are *not* sufficient for ascertaining the truth.

In the original teaching, the Buddha is talking to a clan called the Kalamas. These folks are confused because various gurus have been coming round, trash-talking each other and saying that only their own teachings are right. And so the Kalamas ask the Buddha, "Which of these venerable priests and contemplatives are speaking the truth, and which ones are lying?"

Rather than name names, the Buddha chooses to outline a *method* for determining the truth:

Now, Kalamas, don't go by reports, by legends, by traditions, by scripture, by logical conjecture, by inference, by analogies, by agreement through pondering views, by probability, or by the thought, "This contemplative is our teacher." When you know for yourselves that, "These teachings are skillful; these teachings are blameless; these teachings are praised by the wise; these teachings, when adopted and carried out, lead to welfare and to happiness"—then you should enter and remain in them.

Amongst other things, the Buddha says that "reason" (logical conjecture, inference) and "common sense" (analogies, probability) are not sufficient bases for determining the truth. It's not that these things should be discarded, but that ultimately it's our own experience and observation—and that of the wise—that should act as our guide.

One problem with accepting something only if it agrees with your common sense is that common sense is often wrong. It's common sense to many people that a ten-pound rock will fall faster than a one pound one. It's been common sense to many people over the millennia that the world is flat. And yet neither of these is the case.

Some of the Buddha's teachings, like non-self, actually fly in the face of our common sense. Common sense tells us that we have a self—something that defines us and is the essential "us." But the Buddha taught that there was nothing we could identify as being, in any ultimate sense, a self. This is deeply counterintuitive. The problem is that if we accept only that which agrees with our common sense we end up accepting only that which we are already predisposed to believe.

The first instance of this quote that I've found is in a libertarian book by the pseudonymous John Galt, *Dreams Come Due,* which *Kirkus Reviews* slammed as "a muddled manifesto," noting also that the author presented numerous quotes out of context in order to support his claims. I suspect that Galt altered the Kalama Sutta quote for the same reason.

Incidentally, "no matter where you read it" is an anachronism, since spiritual teachings were orally transmitted at the time of the Buddha. That in itself would make this quote suspect.

9. "Do not dwell in the past, do not dream of the future, concentrate the mind on the present moment."

This quote has its origins in a book called *The Teaching of Buddha* (see also #28, #30, #41). This is a sort of Buddhist Gideon Bible, found in hotels all over Japan and increasingly in the United States as well. It comprises Buddhist scriptures as well as modern commentary, with the two not always being clearly distinguished.

The quote in question is a rendition of verse 348 of the Dhammapada, which literally translates as: "Let go of the past, let go of the future, let go of the present."

"Do not dwell in the past" and "do not dream of the future," although poetic, are close enough, but "concentrate the mind on the present moment" is a significant departure from "let go of the present." The message that past, present, and future should all be treated in the same way gets lost.

It might surprise you to learn that the Buddha rarely talked in terms of "the present moment" or "focusing on the present moment." The language of "being in the moment," "concentrating on the moment," and so on is actually rather modern, with the first examples I've found being from the 1960s.

It's useful language, however. When we're unmindful, we're usually caught up in thinking. And this thinking is usually to do with either the past or the future—for example, when we're resentfully going over some slight from the past or anxiously imagining some future challenge. We can cultivate mindfulness by directing our attention away from such mental time traveling and instead observe whatever is arising—right now—in our direct sensory experience. We observe, for example, whatever sensations are arising from the body, whatever feelings are present, and whatever thoughts the mind is giving rise to. So we talk about this as "being in the moment," "paying attention to the present," and so on.

This terminology can be a bit misleading because it's perfectly possible to reflect on the past or to plan for the future in a mindful way. On the whole, though, it's a helpful way of communicating what we're doing in cultivating mindfulness.

Although many contemporary teachers talk about focusing on the present moment, if you see quotes purporting to be from the Buddha that use that language, I'd suggest being suspicious.

10. 'Ennui has made more gamblers than avarice, more drunkards than thirst, and perhaps as many suicides as despair.'

The polished, literary quality of this quote strongly suggests an origin much more modern than India 2,500 years ago. To get a sense of the style of the early scriptures, here's the Buddha talking about boredom:

> *And what is the food for the arising of unarisen sloth and drowsiness, or for the growth and increase of sloth and drowsiness once it has arisen? There are boredom, weariness, yawning, drowsiness after a meal, and sluggishness of awareness. To foster inappropriate attention to them: This is the food for the arising of unarisen sloth and drowsiness, or for the growth and increase of sloth and drowsiness once it has arisen.*

As well as the repetition, you may also notice the string of near-synonyms ("boredom, weariness, sluggishness"), which helps with memorization but tends—ironically, given the topic—to have a rather yawn-inducing effect on the modern reader.

Ennui is a kind of listless, world-weary boredom, and while boredom was no doubt a problem at the time of the Buddha (perhaps especially for monks and nuns), ennui would be an odd choice of word for a translator to use. To me at least it suggests jaded French aristocrats rather than drowsy meditators.

The quote in question is in reality from the Rev. Caleb Charles Colton's 1820 book, *Lacon: Or, Many Things in Few Words.* Colton was an English cleric and author who's nowadays best known for having coined the familiar phrase, "Imitation is the sincerest form of flattery," which is also something the Buddha never said.

11. 'Every human being is the author of his own health or disease.'

This quote crops up regularly on Twitter, on quote sites, and in many books as well—most of them published since 2005, which shall henceforth be known as "The Year Fact-Checking Died." Because of the polished style and modern language like "human being" and "author," I was immediately suspicious it was fake.

The topic of the quote is *karma*. This is a subject that's widely misunderstood. Karma, in Buddhism, isn't some kind of cosmic judge, meting out rewards and punishments. The word karma literally means "action," although it specifically refers to ethical or unethical actions, as well as to their natural consequences.

The distinction between ethical and unethical actions hinges on the mental states behind them. "Karma, I tell you, is intention," is one of the Buddha's pithier sayings. When we act based on selfish cravings, on the desire to harm others, or out of delusion, we're more likely to experience unpleasant consequences, as well as cause them for others, while happier and more fulfilling outcomes will arise if our actions are based on motivations that are empathetic, compassionate, and wise.

In one passage on the relationship between karma and health, the Buddha says the following:

> *This is the way that leads to long life, that is to say, to have abandoned the killing of living beings, to abstain from killing living beings, to lay aside the rod and lay aside the knife, to be considerate and merciful, and to dwell compassionate for the welfare of all living beings.*

I take this to mean that compassionate states of mind are good for our health—a view that modern psychology supports.

Although the early Buddhist teachings see karma as having an effect on health, I haven't seen any claim from the Buddha that *every* illness we experience is our own fault. In fact he summarized one wrong understanding of karma as the view, "Whatever a person experiences is all caused by what was done in the past." This is a common Hindu teaching on karma, and even though the Buddha condemned it, it's also taught by some Buddhist schools, possibly because of the influence of Hinduism.

While your karmic actions may well affect your health, so might other things. As we all know, actions such as habitually worrying or getting angry might make us more susceptible to getting sick, but no matter how positive we are we might also just pick up a bug that's going round.

The quote in question comes from *Bliss Divine*, by Swami Sivananda, who was indeed a Hindu teacher. As it happens, a significant number of Fake Buddha Quotes are more Hindu than Buddhist in tone.

12. ˙Everything that has a beginning, has an ending. Make your peace with that and all will be well.˙

In the Buddhist discourses a disciple would often have a breakthrough and experience the following insight: "Whatever is subject to origination is all subject to cessation." The start of the quote above seems to be a paraphrase of this in the more accessible language of "beginnings" and "endings."

As I've noted before, it's easier for a Fake Buddha Quote to go into circulation if it has close parallels in Western literature. "Whatever hath a beginning hath also an end" is found in a 1665 book with the superb title, *Another Collection of Philosophical Conferences of the French Virtuosi Upon Questions of All Sorts for the Improving of Natural Knowledg [sic] Made in the Assembly of the Beaux Esprits at Paris by the Most Ingenious Persons of That Nation*. Tweet that!

By 1702, in François Fénelon's *The Lives of the Ancient Philosophers*, this had evolved into the modern form, "Whatever has a beginning has an end."

The quote in question isn't at all un-Buddhist. It's just not one from the Buddha. In fact it comes from Jack Kornfield's *Buddha's Little Instruction Book*, published in 1994. Jack's book contains lots of Buddha-adjacent axioms. Although they're clearly described as "distillations and adaptations" of the Buddha's teaching, they've often been taken by the unwary as scriptural quotations. A year

THE BUDDHA ON FAKE BUDDHA QUOTES

By now you might be thinking something like, "OK, so there are lots of quotes out there that are incorrectly attributed to the Buddha, but wasn't he too spiritual to be bothered about things like that?" Well, if you think of the Buddha as some kind of calm, eternally beatific, "nonjudgmental" being, you might need to brace yourself for a hard impact with reality. The Buddha of the early scriptures is often portrayed as a bad-ass disciplinarian.

One of the things that really seemed to bother him was having words put in his mouth. In an oral culture it was very important to him that his teachings be repeated accurately. And when he was misquoted he responded in very strong terms:

> Monks, these two slander the Tathagata.* Which two? He who explains what was not said or spoken by the Tathagata as said or spoken by the Tathagata. And he who explains what was said or spoken by the Tathagata as not said or spoken by the Tathagata.

At times he used language that was even more pointed. On hearing that his teaching had been misrepresented, his response was often, "And to whom, worthless man, do you understand me to have taught the Teaching like that?"

"Worthless man"? Yikes! You really didn't want to misquote the Buddha in those days!

---

* "Tathagata" is the title that the Buddha most often used to refer to himself. It means "One who is gone [beyond]."

after the book's publication, the *Sun* magazine picked up the quote and, possibly misled by the book title, attributed it to the Buddha. Thus was a Fake Buddha Quote born.

13. 'Happiness does not depend on what you have or who you are, it solely relies on what you think.'

This is another case where the content of the quote contradicts what the Buddha taught. I first came across it in, of all places, the Twitter bio of actress and pop icon Miley Cyrus. My Buddh-dar immediately registered it as not being genuine.

It in fact has its origins in *Steps to the Top*, by American author and motivational speaker "Zig" Ziglar. The original is in a slightly different form: "Remember, happiness doesn't depend upon who you are or what you have; it depends solely upon what you think."

Ziglar was in turn channeling Dale Carnegie's 1936 classic, *How to Win Friends and Influence People*:

It isn't what you have or who you are or

what you are doing that makes you happy or
unhappy. It is what you think about it.

Carnegie's teachings are an expression of
"New Thought," which was a US-born philosophical movement, one of whose central tenets
was that we can free ourselves from suffering by
changing how we think. Keep an eye open for
that term, New Thought. We're going to encounter it again.

Superficially, both Ziglar's and Carnegie's
writings are similar to Buddhism. For example,
the second verse of the Dhammapada says:

Mind precedes all mental states.
Mind is their chief; they are all mind-wrought.
If with a pure mind a person speaks or acts
happiness follows him like his never-departing
shadow.

The difference between this and positive
thinking is that for the Buddha, *citta*, or "mind,"
was much more than "thought." In fact some
translators choose to render *citta* as "heart-mind"
or even just as "heart."

In these verses, the Buddha is talking not
so much about the content of our thoughts but
about the emotional tone of our volitions. Karma

is intention; do we intend to help people or to hurt them? To manipulate them for our own ends or to help them? Do we love them or fear them? Those kinds of distinctions are central to the practice of ethics in Buddhism.

Merely changing our thoughts will, from a Buddhist point of view, bring about only limited change in our lives; it's changing the heart that's key.

14. 'Have compassion for all beings, rich and poor alike; each has their suffering. Some suffer too much, others too little.'

There's nothing at all suspect about the Buddha encouraging us to have compassion for all beings. But the entire point of his teaching was to reduce suffering, and I doubt he would ever have suggested that some people suffer too little.

One of the things that attracted me to explore Buddhism in the first place was its uncompromising nonviolence. In Buddhism there's no room even for righteous anger—as I sometimes have to remind myself. Even, the Buddha said, if a bunch of bandits were to saw you limb from limb, and you had a moment of anger, you wouldn't, *in that*

moment, be practicing his teachings. Any desire
we may have that others suffer is, by definition,
in conflict with the Buddha's teaching.

As the Karaniya Metta Sutta—the Buddha's
best-known teaching on kindness—says:

> *Let no one deceive another*
> *or despise anyone anywhere,*
> *or through anger or resistance*
> *wish for another to suffer.*

I've found our suspect quote on a couple of
internet discussion forums as early as 2006, but
so far nothing before that. Unfortunately, I've no
idea where it originated, but although its birth-
place is obscure, its fakeness is clear.

15. 'Holding on to anger is like drinking poison
     and expecting the other person to die.'

While researching this quote's origins I found
many variations connected one way or another
with the Twelve-step movement. It turned out
that it originated in *The Sermon on the Mount*,
a 1934 book by Emmet Fox, a New York City
church minister.

Fox was a proponent of New Thought (which we came across in regard to quote #13). Amongst other things, New Thought held—or holds, since it exists today under different names—that sickness originates in the mind and that we can heal ourselves by right thinking. It was influenced in its early days by Hindu ideas (see #7, #11, #45). Nowadays, descendents of the original New Thought movement continue as Christian Science, as Law of Attraction teachings, and in the works of popular writers such as Marianne Williamson and Louise Hay.

Many early Alcoholics Anonymous members, including Bill Wilson, the organization's cofounder, used to attend Fox's sermons and read his pamphlets.

The prototype of our fake quote is not exactly pithy:

> *You might as well swallow a dose of Prussic acid in two gulps, and think to protect yourself by saying, "This one is for Robespierre; and this one for the Bristol murderer" [two people who had previously been cited as objects of hatred]. You will hardly have any doubt as to who will receive the benefit of the poison.*

As it was passed down through generations of AA practitioners, this quote became polished by repeated handling. Thus we end up with the quote in question, which is compelling, true, and elegant, but not from the Buddha.

The closest to this in early Buddhist literature isn't from the Buddha either, but from a fifth-century scholar called Buddhaghosa (see also #3). In writing about the futile and self-defeating nature of resentment, Buddhaghosa noted that we are "like a man who wants to hit another and picks up a burning ember or excrement in his hand and so first burns himself or makes himself stink." This, incidentally, is often misattributed to the Buddha as well.

16. 'I never see what has been done; I only see what remains to be done.'

This quote, which is found attributed to the Buddha on many quotes sites and in a number of books, is actually from a letter a young Polish scientific researcher, Maria Skłodowska, wrote to her brother, lamenting the unsatisfactoriness of her scientific and mathematical work:

It is difficult for me to tell you about my life in detail; it is so monotonous and, in fact, so

uninteresting. Nevertheless I have no feeling of
uniformity and I regret only one thing, which
is that the days are so short and that they pass
so quickly. One never notices what has been
done; one can only see what remains to be
done, and if one didn't like the work it would
be very discouraging.

"Who is Maria Skłodowska?" you may ask.
Later she married a Frenchman, discovered
the elements polonium and radium, and was
awarded two Nobel prizes. She is, of course,
Marie Curie.

Even in context it's hard to tell whether this
quote is an expression of perfectionism, where
Curie dismisses her accomplishments and can
focus only on what she hasn't achieved, or
whether it's an expression of the familiar dread
we all experience when new items find their way
onto our to-do list faster than we can check them
off. I suspect that those who believe this to be
a quote by the Buddha think of it as neither of
these, but as an optimistic and visionary statement: *Okay, that's done! On to the next project!*

But it's rather puzzling how this quote should
have become attached to the Buddha in the first
place. Finding out is just one more item on my
own ever-expanding to-do list.

17. *If we could understand a single flower we could understand the whole universe.*

This supposed Buddha quote is an adaptation of something written by the Argentinian literary giant, Jorge Luis Borges: "Tennyson said that if we could understand a single flower we would know who we are and what the world is."

Borges is referring to the following Tennyson poem:

Flower in the crannied wall,
I pluck you out of the crannies;—
Hold you here, root and all, in my hand,
Little flower—but if I could understand
What you are, root and all, and all in all,
I should know what God and man is.

And Tennyson in turn appears to be riffing off of William Blake's "Auguries of Innocence":

To see a World in a Grain of Sand
And Heaven in a Wild Flower
Hold Infinity in the palm of your hand
And Eternity in an hour.

Blake's poem is believed to have been written in 1803, but wasn't published until 1863. Tennyson's poem, which is of course on a very similar theme, was published in … let me see … oh my goodness, it was published in 1863 as well! What a coincidence!

Anyway, to the best of our knowledge, the Buddha never said anything about a flower revealing the workings of the universe, although he did say that the whole world could be understood "just within this fathom-long body," meaning that if you want to understand reality, you can do so by looking closely at the nature of your own experience. That's not a million miles away from Blake's sentiment.

A story about the Buddha composed in China about a thousand years after his death—and almost certainly not based on historical events—depicts the legendary origins of the Zen Buddhist tradition. In this tale the Buddha is sitting in the midst of a gathering of monks. After a long silence, he holds up a flower. One disciple, Mahakashyapa, smiles, showing that he's understood what the Buddha was communicating.

I have no flower to hold up, but I offer you this verse from David Bader's *Zen Judaism*:

To find the Buddha, look within.
Deep inside you are ten thousand flowers.
Each flower blossoms ten thousand times.
Each blossom has ten thousand petals.
You might want to see a specialist.

18. "If you propose to speak, always ask yourself, is it true, is it necessary, is it kind?"

When I first saw this one I thought it might be a paraphrase of something from the scriptures, although it seemed too neat to be a direct quote. But there are close parallels. For example, we're told that there are five factors that mark words as being well spoken:

> It is spoken at the proper time; what is said is true; it is spoken gently; what is said is beneficial; it is spoken with a mind of loving-kindness.

The actual origins of the quote in question lie, however, not in ancient India but in eighteenth-century Britain. The Reverend James Haldane Stewart (1778–1854), who was the son of a Scottish clan chief, is quoted as having advised people to ask themselves before offering criticism, "First, is it true? Second, is it kind? Third, is it necessary?"

The similarity between the scriptural quote and Stewart's is likely due to a kind of religious convergent evolution, since at the time Stewart died the early Buddhist scriptures hadn't even begun to be translated into English.

19. 'If you want to fly, give up everything that weighs you down.'

This quote's an adaptation from a Toni Morrison novel, *Song of Solomon*: "Can't nobody fly with all that shit. Wanna fly, you got to give up the shit that weighs you down." This statement is ostensibly in reference to why a peacock's tail renders it unable to fly, although of course it's loaded with symbolism.

Whoever first thought to pass this off as a quote from the Buddha made a wise choice in dropping the word "shit," which would have been a dead giveaway.

20. 'If your compassion does not include yourself it is incomplete.'

This quote immediately struck me as suspect because although the Buddha talked a lot about having compassion for others, he had very little to say about self-compassion. His perspective seems to have been that having compassion for ourselves is natural; our task is to extend it to others.

For self-hating Westerners, this might seem odd. How could ancient Indians have been so much at peace with themselves? Actually, self-hatred wasn't entirely unknown. On at least one occasion the Buddha commented on people not liking themselves:

Even though they may say, 'We aren't dear to ourselves,' still they are dear to themselves. Why is that? Of their own accord, they act toward themselves as a dear one would act toward a dear one; thus they are dear to themselves.

So we may *say* we don't like ourselves, but if we're taking care of our own well-being—which most of us do pretty well—we're relating to ourselves as a friend. Do you buy your enemies coffee beverages anytime they feel like a treat, and splurge on nice phones and wide-screen TVs to make sure that they're entertained? Probably not.

If you're affected by self-hatred, perhaps one of the things you could do is to notice the many ways in which you do actually take care of yourself—even simple things like crossing the road safely—and appreciate that these are acts of kindness.

This quote is actually another from *Buddha's Little Instruction Book*, by Jack Kornfield (see also #12, #36). The book's title has led many people to think that it's a book of scriptural quotations, even though it describes itself as a "distillation and adaptation" of sayings from many sources.

21. 'In order to gain anything you must lose everything.'

I have a near-fatherly fondness for this quote, having virtually seen its birth. In April 2010, PBS aired a special called *The Buddha*, narrated by Richard Gere. Referring to the legend of the Buddha-to-be renouncing a life of wealth, comfort, and sensual pleasure in order to seek spiritual awakening, the poet Jane Hirshfield commented, "In order to gain anything, you must first lose everything." (Hirshfield may have been unaware she was paraphrasing the 1999 film *Fight Club*, where the character Tyler Durden says, "It's only after we've lost everything that we're free to do anything.")

Someone who evidently liked Hirshfield's quote tweeted it (slightly altered) and so "In order to gain anything you must lose everything" now appears frequently as a Buddha quote on social media and even on T-shirts, sweatshirts, and onesies.

At the same time, another viewer inexplicably misheard the quote as "To gain *heart* you must lose everything" and tweeted that version, which also continues to circulate on social media, years later, despite (to me at least) not having any obvious meaning. It seems that it's remarkably easy to just make something up, stick the Buddha's name at the end of it, and have it be taken seriously, no matter how nonsensical it may be.

Loss, the Buddha repeatedly pointed out, is inevitable. In a number of passages he asked us to reflect on the fact that we will at some point be separated from everything we hold dear. The point of such reflections is to lessen the pain that arises from assuming that the objects of our affections will always be with us (or we with them). And it's in losing this assumption of permanence that true happiness will be found:

> *Even if a person lives a century—or more— he's parted from his community of relatives, he abandons his life right here ...*

> *Seeking your own happiness, you should pull out your own arrow: your own lamentation, longing, and sorrow.*

The Buddhist emphasis on nonattachment misleads some into thinking that the goal of Buddhist practice is to become uncaring, but that's far from the case. On the one hand we're encouraged to remember the impermanence of our connections with others, while on the other we're reminded to love all beings as a mother loves her only child (see #32).

22. 'In the confrontation between the stream and the rock, the stream always wins; not through strength, but through perseverance.'

The oldest instance of this that I've found is in H. Jackson Brown's 1988 quote compilation, *A Father's Book of Wisdom*, where it's attributed to his own dad.

The basic notion of water's long-term victory over rock is an ancient one. In Ovid's *Ars Amatoria* there's a couplet that translates as:

What is more hard than stone, what is softer than the wave?
Nevertheless, the hard stones are worn away by the soft water.

I haven't found this metaphor being used by the Buddha, although he did talk about the persistence of water drops:

Think not lightly of good, saying, "It will not come to me." Drop by drop is the water pot filled. Likewise, the wise man, gathering it little by little, fills himself with good.[37]

Okay, not quite the same thing. The Chinese Taoist tradition, which has much in common with Buddhism, comes closer. In the Tao Te Ching there's a very relevant quote:

Nothing under heaven is softer or more yielding than water, but when it attacks things hard and resistant there is not one of them that can prevail.

While we're on the theme of erosion, there's an interesting image that the Buddha used to help us get our heads around the immense age of the universe:

There is a huge rock which is seven miles by the length, breadth, and the height. It is without a flaw, not perforated and of the same thickness everywhere. After the lapse of one hundred thousand years a man comes with a cashmere cloth and touches the rock once. By this method the rock diminishes and vanishes, but the world cycle does not come to an end.

In the confrontation between the rock and the handkerchief, the handkerchief will win. But it's going to take a while.

23. ˙In the sky there is no distinction of east and west; people create the distinctions out of their own minds and then believe them to be true.˙

The Buddha did use metaphors involving the sky, but this particular quote doesn't ring true. Sure enough, the original source is *The Teaching of Buddha,* the Gideon Bible–type publication from which have sprung several spurious quotes (see #9, #28, #30, #41).

If I quote the passage more fully, you'll recognize that it's not the kind of thing you'd expect to find in a 2,500-year-old scripture:

In the sky there is no distinction of east and west; people create the distinctions out of their

own minds and then believe them to be true.
Mathematical numbers from one to infinity are
each complete numbers, and each in itself car-
ries no distinction of quantity; but people make
the discrimination for their own convenience, so
as to be able to indicate varying amounts.

Only a mention of quantum physics could render it more obvious that this isn't a genuine Buddha quote.

This passage is a paraphrase of something written by Nichiren Daishonin, a Japanese teacher from the thirteenth century. Nichiren talked about verbal distinctions such as "heaven and earth, big and small, east and west," and so on, and immediately after says "Outside of the mind there are neither distinctions nor the absence of distinctions."

There's a passage in the Dhammapada (verse 92) that uses the image of the sky as a symbol of indefinability.

Those whose field is freedom, void and indefin-
able, their trail, like that of birds through the
sky, can't be traced.

Our minds, in an attempt to give us a sense of security in an ever-changing, inconstant world, are always trying to define us and the world around us. As the quote in question says, we create distinctions and take them to be absolute.

The awakened mind, on the other hand, totally at peace with itself, holds onto nothing, tries to define nothing, and is entirely at home in a world of change, just as a bird is at home in the formlessness of the sky.

Once again, the quote isn't wrong, even if the attribution to the Buddha is.

WHAT IS A GENUINE BUDDHA QUOTE?

In a sense, there's no such thing as a "genuine" Buddha quote. The earliest scriptures we have were passed down orally for hundreds of years before being committed to writing. What was transmitted was simplified, edited, and made repetitious so that it would be easier to memorize through chanting. So there's no way to guarantee that any particular sentence is recorded exactly as the Buddha uttered it.

So if there's no such thing as a 100 percent guaranteed, for-sure, no-doubt-about-it Genuine Buddha Quote, then how can there be such a thing as a Fake Buddha Quote? Well, we don't have to be certain about what the Buddha did say in order to know what he didn't say. The Buddha's own rule was that if you can't find a quote in the scriptures you should regard it as fake:

24. 'It is better to travel well than to arrive.'

Although we might think about monks and nuns being settled in monasteries, at the time of the Buddha they were generally on the move from village to village, teaching, and living on food that they begged going from door to door—in the same way, as one of the Buddha's sayings has it, that bees gathered nectar by going from flower

Without approval and without scorn, but carefully studying the sentences word by word, one should trace them in the Discourses and verify them by the Discipline. If they are neither traceable in the Discourses nor verifiable by the Discipline, one must conclude thus: "Certainly, this is not the Blessed One's utterance; this has been misunderstood by that monk—or by that community, or by those elders, or by that elder." In that way, monks, you should reject it.

If there's no evidence of the Buddha having said something, then we can't legitimately claim he did. Additionally, if something being passed around on Facebook can be definitively tracked down to a source that isn't the historical Buddha (say Madame Curie or Toni Morrison), then that's an obvious misattribution, and should be regarded as fake.

to flower. The Buddha, in other words, did a lot of traveling.

However, the quote above isn't something the Buddha said. It's an adaptation of something by the Scottish author Robert Louis Stevenson, perhaps most famous for the classics *Treasure Island* and *The Strange Case of Dr. Jekyll and Mr. Hyde*. In an 1881 essay, "El Dorado," he wrote, "Little do ye know your own blessedness, for to travel hopefully is a better thing than to arrive, and the true success is to labour."

It was only around 2004 that the simplified version of the quote above first became ascribed to the Buddha.

25. 'It is possible to live happily in the present moment. It is the only moment we have.'

As I've mentioned before (see #9), the Buddha didn't talk in terms of the rather modern idiom of "being in the moment," so I hope you're primed to be suspicious of this quote, which is actually from the Vietnamese Buddhist teacher Thich Nhat Hanh.

In *No Death, No Fear*, Thay, as he's known to his disciples, writes:

The Buddha said, "It is possible to live happily in the present moment. It is the only moment we have."

Elsewhere he equates the phrase "It is possible to live happily in the present moment" with an expression that translates as "abiding in ease, here and now" or "a pleasant abiding here and now" (*dittha-dhamma-sukha-vihara*). This refers to the way in which the benefits of meditation and other spiritual practices are not deferred until after death, or even to some future date in this lifetime, but can be experienced *right now*, in this very moment.

Now it's certainly possible to render the original Pali as "living happily in the present moment," but not in the form "It is *possible* to live happily in the present moment," which would require a completely different form of grammar (namely a verb in the optative mood). And there's nothing in the original phrase corresponding to "it is the only moment we have."

When a book is compiled from talks, as many of Thay's are, errors can creep in. I have a hunch he said something like, "The Buddha said it is possible to 'live happily in the present moment.' This is the only moment we have." Only the part in single quotes would have been a quotation, but it's possible that the transcriber or editor mistakenly took everything after the words "The Buddha said" as a direct speech.

However, the statement that the present is the only moment we have is in line with what the Buddha taught:

Let not a person revive the past
Or on the future build his hopes,
For the past has been left behind
And the future has not been reached.

26. ˙Let us rise up and be thankful, for if we didn't learn a lot today, at least we learned a little.˙

This one puzzled me when I saw it. The diction is unlike anything you'd see in any Buddhist scripture from any era. And "rise up"? What's that all about? Levitating? Starting a revolution?

Anyway, the original source is Leo Buscaglia, also known as "Dr. Love," who was an American author, university professor, and motivational speaker. In his 1992 book, *Born for Love*, he wrote:

Years ago I had a Buddhist teacher in Thailand who would remind all his students that there was always something to be thankful for. He'd say, "Let's rise and be thankful, for if we didn't learn a lot today, at least we may have learned a little. And if we didn't learn even a little, at least we didn't get sick. And if we did get sick, at least we didn't die. So let us all be thankful."

I imagine this being said at the end of a talk or meditation session, which would explain the "rise up" part.

The Buddha was pro-thankfulness, of course. He said things like: "These two people are hard to find in the world. Which two? The one who is first to do a kindness, and the one who is grateful for a kindness done."

And to my mind one of the funniest passages in the scriptures goes like this:

Monks, did you hear an old jackal howling at the flush of dawn? ... There may be some gratitude and thankfulness in that old jackal, but there is no gratitude and thankfulness in a certain person here claiming to be one of my followers.

And that, ladies and gentleman, is what the kids nowadays call "a sick burn."

27. 'Life has no meaning in itself but it is itself an opportunity to make it meaningful.'

The idiom of life having meaning is relatively modern. The earliest instance I've found so far is in the Scottish thinker Thomas Carlyle's *Sartor Resartus* (see also #37), published in 1831: "Our Life is compassed round with Necessity; yet is the meaning of Life itself no other than Freedom."[48] The expression may well be a bit older, but I hope you get the point: it's not the way people talked 2,500 years ago.

The origins of the quote probably lie in something written by Osho, aka the Bhagwan Shree Rajneesh (see also #29), who has been referred to as a "neo-Hindu" teacher. Rajneesh had a huge following in the West. He was famous for accumulating numerous white Rolls Royces and for his commune in Oregon having launched the first biological terror attack in modern US history. Not surprisingly, Osho was deported from the United States after this incident, and his commune collapsed.

In a book with the strange title *Dang Dang Doko Dang*, he says, "Life has no meaning in itself, you have to bring meaning into it. Life is just raw material, you have to create your meaning out of it."

One of the Buddha's chief disciples, Sariputta, once said that "The holy life is lived under the Blessed One with the purpose (*attha*) of knowing, seeing, attaining, realizing, and breaking through to what has been unknown, unseen, unattained, unrealized, and not broken through to."

You'll notice that our job is not to create this purpose but instead to know, see, realize, and break through into it. Perhaps our purpose doesn't need to be created, because it's already there?

28. 'Meditate. Live purely. Be quiet. Do your work with mastery. Like the moon, come out from behind the clouds! Shine.'

This is another quote from Thomas Byrom's version of the Dhammapada (see also #7, #45), and it actually comprises two separate passages that have been thrust together.

The first part, "Meditate. Live purely. Be quiet. Do your work with mastery," corresponds to Dhammapada verse 386. In Buddharakkhita's rigorously literal translation, this is:

He who is meditative, stainless and settled, whose work is done and who is free from cankers, having reached the highest goal—him do I call a holy man.

There's not much resemblance between this and Byrom's attempt.

The second part corresponds to Dhammapada verse 382, which Buddharakkhita translates as:

That monk who while young devotes himself to the Teaching of the Buddha illumines this world like the moon freed from clouds.

Compare this to "Like the moon, come out from behind the clouds! Shine." It may be no accident that Byrom's publisher avoids calling his book a translation, opting for the more accurate "rendering."

I have to assume that Byrom worked from existing translations, plucked a few words from them, and then fabricated a new quote that said what he wanted the Buddha to say. It's as if I were to take the opening of Shakespeare's Sonnet 18,

Shall I compare thee to a summer's day?
Thou art more lovely and more temperate.
Rough winds do shake the darling buds of May,
And summer's lease hath all too short a date.

and to render it as a "Shakespeare Quote" like this:

Like the sun, let your beauty shine. Find balance. Open like a bud trembling in the wind. Remember: all things pass.

What do you think? Should I have a go at Hamlet next?

29. 'My doctrine is not a doctrine but just a vision. I have not given you any set rules, I have not given you a system.'

Yikes! That's *way* too contemporary to be the Buddha. In fact it's another one from Osho, the guru formerly known as Bhagwan Shree Rajneesh (see also: #27).

The quote is from Osho's commentary on the Diamond Sutra, where he's referring to the following passage:

This Dharma which the Tathagata [Buddha] has fully known or demonstrated—it cannot be grasped, it cannot be talked about, it is neither a Dharma nor a no-Dharma.

This is a rather mysterious—and lovely—way of restating the idea that Reality is "beyond concepts" and that the Buddha's teaching is nothing more than a raft (see #1) to get us to the far shore of insight that lies across the river of delusion that's just west of the superhighway of metaphor.

Here's Osho's commentary:

A doctrine is a set, fixed phenomenon. The universe is in flux; no doctrine can contain it. No doctrine can be just to it, no doctrine can do justice to existence. All doctrines fall short.

So Buddha says: "My doctrine is not a doctrine but just a vision. I have not given you any set rules, I have not given you a system."

For what it's worth, I think Osho's explanation is excellent. But he's paraphrasing what he understood the Buddha's message to have been, rather than quoting him. It's understandable, though, that someone might think that these words were being presented as a verbatim quote from the Buddha and decide to pass them on as such (see also #9, #25).

30. 'On the long journey of human life, faith is the best of companions; it is the best refreshment on the journey; and it is the greatest property.'

This is another quote from *The Teaching of Buddha* (see also #9, #23, #28, #41), which is published by a Japanese missionary organization and found, apparently, in every hotel room in Japan.

The Teaching of Buddha has been in continuous publication since at least the 1930s. My own copy is from 1985, and it's the 115th edition! There are some scriptural passages in there, but a lot of it is composed of non-scriptural writings. It's quite clear from the context in the book that this quote's not being presented as the Buddha's words. What may have happened here is that someone saw a quote with the attribution "The Teaching of Buddha" and assumed it was straight from the Buddha's mouth.

When the Buddha referred to the rounds of rebirth he did in fact refer to life as a "long journey" (*dighena addhuna*). But he tended to emphasize an individual human life as being short. For example he said, "Life is difficult and brief and bound up with suffering." Reflections like these weren't intended to depress us, but to help us appreciate the fleeting and precious time we have upon this earth, so that we may make something worthwhile of it.

Life is short! Make every moment meaningful!

31. "Place no head above your own."

You might be tempted to take this quote to mean that you shouldn't revere anyone or regard them as being better than yourself. However, that's not what this saying is about. Nor is it from the Buddha.

It's actually by the ninth-century Zen master Linji (also known as Rinzai), who said,

> *Just what are you seeking in the highways and byways? Blind men! You're putting a head on top of the one you already have. What do you yourselves lack? ... You just don't believe this and keep on seeking outside.*

Putting a head on top of the one you already have means seeing the world through the lens of someone else's experience rather than using your own experience as a basis for insight. It's a useful and witty quote. It's just not from the Buddha.

One word the Buddha used to describe his teaching was *ehipassiko*, which literally means "come and see." He intended his teaching to be directly practiced and experienced rather than merely understood or believed in.

32. "Resolve to be tender with the young, compassionate with the aged, sympathetic with the striving, and tolerant with the weak and wrong. Sometime in your life, you will have been all of these."

Garson O'Toole of the Quote Investigator website beat me to the punch on this one, showing that it's actually from Lloyd Shearer, who wrote "Walter Scott's Personality Parade" for *Parade* magazine from 1958 to 1991. (A minor point: in the original quote it's "tolerant *of*" the weak and wrong, rather than "tolerant *with*.")

One of the best-known Buddhist teachings on love, the Karaniya Metta Sutta (see #14), is similar in that it encourages us to have an empathetic and compassionate approach to beings of all kinds:

> *Whatever living beings there may be,*
> *Whether fearful or self-possessed,*
> *Without exception,*
> *Whether large, great, middling, or small,*
> *Whether tiny or substantial,*
> *Whether seen or unseen,*
> *Whether living near or far,*
> *Born or unborn;*
> *May all beings be happy.*
> *Let none deceive or despise another anywhere.*
> *Let none wish harm to another,*
> *In anger or in hate.*

In the Buddha's teaching, empathy doesn't depend on us having been all the types of beings we're encouraged to develop kindness toward. What's important is to cultivate an empathetic awareness that other beings' happiness and suffering are as real to them as ours are to us, and therefore to treat them with respect and kindness.

As one of the Buddha's teachings says, "What is displeasing and disagreeable to me is displeasing and disagreeable to the other, too. How can I inflict upon another what is displeasing and disagreeable to me?"

33. "Success is not the key to happiness;
    happiness is the key to success. If you love
    what you are doing, you will be successful."

The person who sent me this said that it sounded
so "Zig Ziglar-ish" (see #13) that he couldn't
imagine the Buddha saying anything even
remotely like it. I agreed.

The rhetorical flourish used here is called a
chiasmus. John F. Kennedy's "Ask not what your
country can do for you; ask what you can do for
your country" is another example.

The quote in question is often ascribed to
either the Buddha or Albert Schweitzer. So
far, the oldest instance that I've found is in an
interview with Herman Cain, in a 1996 issue
of *Parade* magazine (which was also the source of
quote #32). Cain, an African-American busi-
nessman who went on to run as a Republican
presidential candidate, probably deserves the
credit for having coined this expression.

Depending on how we interpret "success," I
think the Buddha would have largely agreed with
the first part of this quote, since he saw happiness
as an important aspect of the path to Awakening.
A common pattern in the Buddha's teachings,
outlined in various degrees of detail depending
on the circumstances, is that living ethically leads

to freedom from remorse, and therefore to happiness; that happiness leads to a mind that is free from conflict and thus able to remain calm and concentrated; and that a concentrated mind has the kind of focused attention necessary in order to develop insight. So if "success" is defined in terms of awakening, then it's certainly true that happiness is one of the keys to success, even if the Buddha never quite put it that way.

But inherent in this is a critique of the second part of the quote: "If you love what you are doing, you will be successful." The Buddha would consider that only if what you love doing is ethical could it be a fit basis for a truly happy life.

34. "Suffering is not holding you. You are holding suffering."

I've seen this one in a few places purporting to be from the Buddha. Actually it's an adaptation of something Osho (see also #27, #29) wrote in his book *The Voice of Silence*:

> *I say to you that suffering is not holding onto you, you are holding onto suffering ... one day you will realize that you were dragging it*

*around with you—and no one except you was
responsible for this. Whatever suffering you
experienced, nobody else was to blame. It was
your wish, you wanted to suffer.*

The world of Fake Buddha Quotes apparently
being rather small, Osho's book is a commentary
on *Light on the Path*, by the theosophist Mabel
Collins, which is the source of quote #48.

The Buddha of course had a lot to say about
suffering, since that's what his teachings have
the purpose of liberating us from. He does
suggest that we cling to suffering, as when in a
well-known discourse he says of the "worldling"
(*puthujjana*, see #3), "Sensing a feeling of pain,
he senses it as though joined with it."

In the same teaching he points out, using a
very neat analogy, that much of our suffering is
caused by our reactions to pain:

*Just as if they were to shoot a man with an arrow
and, right afterward, were to shoot him with
another one, so that he would feel the pains of
two arrows; in the same way, when touched with
a feeling of pain, the uninstructed run-of-the-
mill person [puthujjana] sorrows, grieves, and
laments, beats his breast, becomes distraught. So
he feels two pains, physical and mental.*

Mindfulness—that is, the activity of observing our experience rather than merely being caught up in it—allows us to sense pain not as something we're joined to and immersed in, but as a separate object of attention. And this observational stance helps us to refrain from grieving, sorrowing, and lamenting, so that we don't cause ourselves extra, unnecessary suffering.

I've seen no indication that the Buddha thought that deep down we want to suffer, though, and in fact that view smacks of a "blame the victim" mentality. Rather, it seems that we want to avoid suffering, but blinded by ignorance, we run headlong into it. Shantideva, a teacher from the eighth century, sums this up very neatly:

Hoping to escape suffering, it is to suffering that they run. In the desire for happiness, out of delusion, they destroy their own happiness, like an enemy.

35. 'The Dharma that I preach can be understood only by those who know how to think.'

This one, which is found quite often on Facebook, blogs, and so on, didn't ring true to me.

This quote is probably a sloppy paraphrase of one of two things the Buddha said. The first is that the Dharma is "to be realized by the wise for themselves," and the other is that it's "beyond the scope of conjecture …to be experienced by the wise."

While clear thinking is a useful and necessary quality, ultimately the Dharma (truth, reality) is beyond concepts (see #1, #29). We can't think our way to Awakening. Reality is something to be experienced and seen.

The quote in question might be part of an attempt to make Buddhism seem rationalistic and therefore more palatable to modern readers. We've seen a similar attempt in regard to quote #8, which emphasized that we should only accept teachings that accord with reason and common sense.

Reason and common sense are excellent and even indispensable tools, but the Buddha advocated an approach that was primarily experiential. To be more in line with what the Buddha taught, perhaps this quote should read, "The Dharma that I preach can be understood only by those who know how to *look*."

36. "The heart is like a garden: it can grow
    compassion or fear, resentment or love.
    What seeds will you plant there?"

By now I hope you recognize that this is nothing
like the style of teaching found in the Buddhist
scriptures. In fact, it's another one from Jack
Kornfield's *Buddha's Little Instruction Book* (see
also #12, #20).

But even if the idiom isn't right, Kornfield's
message is actually very Buddhist in spirit. The
Buddha emphasized that we all make choices
that lead to different consequences, and he
sometimes used the simile of seeds to illustrate
this. He talked about how, just as some kinds of
seeds lead to bitter fruits, so certain actions lead
to suffering. And there are wholesome seeds that
lead to more palatable consequences:

> *Just as when a sugar cane seed, a rice grain, or
> a grape seed is placed in moist soil, whatever
> nutriment it takes from the soil and the water,
> all conduces to its sweetness, tastiness, and
> unalloyed delectability ... In the same way,
> when a person has [skillful qualities conducive
> to awakening], all lead to what is agreeable,
> pleasing, charming, profitable, and easeful.*

It's hard to be sure, but it may be that Kornfield paraphrased this very quotation in order to come up with his rather lovely image.

37. 'The instant we feel anger we have already ceased striving for the truth, and have begun striving for ourselves.'

As soon as I saw this one, it struck me as being off. The language of "striving for ourselves" is too idiomatic and modern for the Buddha. My first clue in tracking down its origins was an essay, "Voltaire," by the Scottish philosopher and author, Thomas Carlyle (see also #27):

> A wise man has well reminded us, that "in any controversy, the instant we feel angry, we have already ceased striving for Truth, and begun striving for Ourselves."*

But who is the "wise man" Carlyle is quoting? According to *Day's Collacon* (1884), and William

---

* Note that instead of "angry," the version ascribed to the Buddha has "anger," which certainly sounds more Buddha-like, and has "the truth" rather than Truth.

Macdonald Sinclair's *Simplicity in Christ* (1896), these are the words of the Rev. Archibald Alison of Edinburgh, who lived from 1757 to 1839 and who was a friend of Robert Burns, Scotland's national poet. Carlyle heard Alison preach in Edinburgh, and praised his elocution and style.

So far I haven't managed to locate Alison's *Essay on the Nature and Principles of Taste*, or his two volumes of sermons, published in 1814, to find the quote in his writings. This may not be what he said. But I'm certain that it isn't from the Buddha.

38. 'The only real failure in life is not to be true to the best one knows.'

I encountered this quote in a Huffington Post article by Deb and Ed Shapiro, entitled "What the Buddha Might Say to President Obama." It wouldn't have been the Buddha who said this to the former US President, however, but Frederic William Farrar, an Indian-born Dean of Canterbury who lived from 1831 to 1903. The quote is from Farrar's book, *Success In Life*, published in 1885, although the wording there is slightly different: "There is but one failure; and that is, not to be true to the best one knows."

I think I'd have liked Frederic. He believed that everyone was headed to heaven eventually, and he also argued against the notion that one of the perks of being there is having the eternal torment of souls in hell as a spectator sport. He was also one of Charles Darwin's pall-bearers, which strikes me as a brave thing for a religious man to do at that time.

When quotations are anonymous or by people who are no longer well known, it's common for them to be reassigned to more famous figures, which is what has happened here. I predict that in the distant future all quotes from our era will be attributed to Mark Twain, Winston Churchill, Albert Einstein—and of course the Buddha.

The Buddha offered a neat teaching—a kind of Dharma domino theory—on how failure stems from the embrace of mistaken views:

> *In a person of wrong view, wrong resolve comes into being. In a person of wrong resolve, wrong speech. In a person of wrong speech, wrong action. In a person of wrong action, wrong livelihood. In a person of wrong livelihood, wrong effort. In a person of wrong effort, wrong mindfulness. In a person of wrong mindfulness, wrong concentration. In a person of wrong concentration, wrong knowledge. In a person of*

WE'RE ALL THE BUDDHA...

Many people have written to me telling me why it's misguided to point out that the Buddha didn't say some of the things people claim he said. One of the most interesting reasons they give is that "we're all the Buddha," and so all of these quotes whose attributions I debunk are "really" Buddha quotes.

There are indeed some schools of Buddhism that say that we all have "Buddha Nature"—that enlightenment lies within all of us. What this means varies. Sometimes it just means we all have the potential to awaken, while other times it means that Reality is a kind of "ground of being" that pervades us all.

If we're to say that "Buddha is in all of us" and *therefore* that anything anyone says can be meaningfully attributed to the historical Buddha, Shakyamuni, then the historical Buddha, Shakyamuni, presumably then said, "Ich bin ein Berliner," although conventionally speaking we would attribute this to John F. Kennedy. He also presumably said, "All happy families are alike; each unhappy family is unhappy in its own way" (which is the opening line of his novel *Anna Karenina*). Additionally, the Buddha is responsible for, "It is not truth that matters, but victory," although some would insist that this was actually by Adolf Hitler.

Personally, though, I don't see the logic in saying that because we are all potentially enlightened, then we can therefore ascribe anything we want to the historical individual, Shakyamuni. It's a bit like saying that since every American child has the potential to become the president, I can preface something my child said with the words, "As the president remarked this morning . . ." It makes no sense as an argument and leads to the absurdities I've highlighted above.

We can't tell for sure whether the Buddha said all the things ascribed to him in the early scriptures (although they remain our best bet for authenticity), but we can tell when things ascribed to him were actually said by someone else, or are in some way foreign to the canon. As we've seen, some of the quotes wrongly attributed to the Buddha are very much in line with what he taught, and the main issue I see there is whether we care about accuracy (I'll have more to say about that in the conclusion). But some Fake Buddha Quotes are highly misleading.

The Buddha described his teaching as being like a set of directions leading to an ancient city that he had discovered hidden deep in the forest. If some of the instructions say "go South" when actually we're meant to head North, we might end up wasting years of our time following the wrong path.

wrong knowledge, wrong release. This is how from wrongness comes failure, not success.

Failure comes from not practicing the eight-fold path (view through concentration), since this leads to wrong knowledge and wrong (that is, non-) release. So for the Buddha, just as for William Farrar, failure comes from not being true to the best one knows.

39. 'The secret of happiness lies in the mind's release from worldly ties.'

A reader of my blog spotted this quote in one of Molly Hahn's "Buddha Doodles," which are charming and whimsical watercolor cartoons, sometimes accompanied by quotes. Quite a few of the quotes Hahn attributes to the Buddha are fake, however.

This particular one is another bad paraphrase—a "lost in translation quote." The Buddha did of course talk about happiness, but not of the "secret of happiness," which is a relatively modern expression. This quote comes from an article in the British Buddhist Society's journal, *The Middle Way*, from February 1974, which includes a slightly different version of the quote in the form of a couplet:

> *The secret of happiness lies*
> *In mind's release from worldly ties*

There is an actual scripture being referred to here, which centers on a discussion between the Buddha and Hatthaka, one of his disciples. Hatthaka is having trouble understanding how the Buddha, who owns nothing, can be happy. In the translation by Bhikkhu Bodhi, a well-respected modern scholar-monk, this verse is:

> *Having cut off all attachments,*
> *having removed anguish in the heart,*
> *the peaceful one sleeps well,*
> *having attained peace of mind.*

This is a much more complex statement than the couplet above, and of course there's no reference to a "secret of happiness." But the other translator of this passage, whom I haven't yet been able to identify, evidently wanted to end with a rhyme, and had to radically alter the wording in order to achieve that end.

The change may not seem major, but the expression "the secret of happiness" is very alien to the way the Buddha expressed himself and makes him sound like a modern self-help guru.

40. ˙The whole secret of existence is to have no fear.˙

And so we move from the "secret of happiness" to the "secret of existence."

This quote is actually from a talk given to a small group of disciples by the Hindu teacher Swami Vivekananda in July 1895 on Thousand Island, New York.* The fact that the talk was delivered over a century ago made me wonder when people started talking about a "secret of existence." It struck me as being a very nine-teenth-century expression.

A search on Google Books's admittedly rather patchy archive gave only one instance of that phrase from the 1700s and one more from 1800 to 1820, but dozens from 1820 to 1830, which is when this phrase seems to have come into vogue. The phrase "secret of life" is found

---

* Yes, that's the same Thousand Island that the salad dressing is named after.

in books throughout the 1700s. Even earlier, going as far back as the 1500s, was the phrase "secret of nature."

Nowadays people are more likely to talk about a secret of happiness or of success rather than existence. But if you can buy the secrets of longevity, of unlocking hidden dimensions of your inner life, and of closing the deal on Amazon, how secret can they be?

Although the phrase "secret of existence" doesn't seem to have been in use 2,500 years ago, the Buddha was often described as someone who had metaphorically held "an oil lamp in the dark so that those with eyes may see," and as one who had "revealed what had been hidden." He was in a sense a revealer of the secrets of existence, he just didn't use that expression.

41.   'There is nothing more dreadful than the habit of doubt.'

This was sent to me as part of a longer quote:

> *There is nothing more dreadful than the habit of doubt. Doubt separates people. It is a poison that disintegrates friendships and breaks up*

pleasant relations. It is a thorn that irritates and hurts; it is a sword that kills.

This is from a 1934 book by the American author and pioneer of Western Buddhism, Dwight Goddard. The book's title is *Buddha, Truth and Brotherhood: An Epitome of Many Buddhist Scriptures, Translated from the Japanese.* We've actually encountered this work before, since this was the title given to an early American edition of *The Teaching of Buddha* (see also #9, #28, #30).

The passage continues, "The beginnings of faith were planted by the compassion of Buddha, long, long ago. When one has faith he should realize this fact and be very grateful to Buddha for his goodness," which pretty much puts to rest the notion that this is a quote from the Buddha himself.

The word "doubt" in the Buddhist scriptures doesn't have the modern connotation of honest skepticism, incidentally—it refers to a state of low confidence and confusion.

The mind that is full of doubt is compared by the Buddha to a pot of muddy water:

Imagine a bowl of water, agitated, stirred up, muddied, put in a dark place. If a man with good eyesight were to look at the reflection of his own face in it, he would not know or see it as it really was. In the same way, priest, when a man dwells with his heart possessed and overwhelmed by doubt-and-wavering … then he cannot know or see, as it really is, what is to his own profit, to the profit of others, to the profit of both.

The Buddha did indeed regard this kind of doubt as a dreadful "habit." In Buddhist teaching it's one of the five hindrances to meditative absorption, one of the first three fetters that hold us back from stream entry (the first level of awakening), and one of the seven underlying tendencies to unskillful behavior (or *anusayas* in Pali).

The opposite of doubt, as Goddard's words make clear, is faith (*saddha*). In Buddhism, rather than being a form of blind belief, faith is a form of trust or confidence that is based on experience. We'll learn a bit more about faith in the context of the next quote.

42. ˙To force oneself to believe and to accept a thing without understanding is political, and not spiritual or intellectual.˙

As you may have gathered by now, the Buddha didn't talk like a twentieth-century highbrow.

This quote is actually from the Sri Lankan Buddhist monk, scholar, and writer Walpola Rahula's well-known book, *What the Buddha Taught*.

I wholeheartedly agree with what Rahula has to say, incidentally. When we say "I believe" with regard to something that we can't verify from direct experience, we're often essentially saying "I choose to align myself with this group as opposed to another."

Buddhism is not principally a system of belief, but of practice; it's not about what you believe, but about what you do. As I've explained before, in Buddhist psychology the word "faith" represents trust or confidence based on experience. Faith is like following someone's instructions on how to get from point A to point B in an unfamiliar place; once you've discovered for yourself that the first few directions correspond to reality, you can begin to trust your guide. This trust is *saddha*—faith.

Rahula points out that the Buddha encouraged his disciples to voice their doubts or uncertainties about the teaching, and said that if it was out of respect for him, the teacher, that they didn't ask questions, they should get a friend to ask for them. It's this spirit of openness and inquiry that attracted me to Buddhist practice in the first place.

43. "To understand everything is to forgive
    everything."

Although this was first shared as a quote from
the Buddha as early as 1910, most sources attribute it to the magnificently accomplished French
author and thinker Germaine de Staël (1766–
1817), who jousted intellectually and politically
with Napoleon.

But the words above aren't exactly what de
Staël wrote. In her novel *Corinne* she actually
said, "For to understand everything makes one
tolerant, and to feel deeply inspires great kindness."* The version we have today is yet another
reminder of how quotes become more polished,
pithy, and punchy as they are handed down from
generation to generation.

Rather than talk in terms of the positive quality of forgiveness, the Buddha more often talked
about having an absence of angry thoughts, as in
this verse from the Dhammapada:

> *"He abused me, he struck me, he overpowered
> me, he robbed me." Those who do not harbor
> such thoughts still their hatred.*

---

* *"Car tout comprendre rend très indulgent, et sentir profondément
inspire une grande bonté."*

Forgiveness is sometimes explicitly mentioned though:

These two are wise people. Which two? The one who sees his transgression as a transgression, and the one who rightfully pardons another who has confessed his transgression.

We'll naturally tend to interpret the "understand everything" version of the Madame de Staël quote as being about empathetically understanding others' situations, motivations, and so on. Curiously, there seems to be very little along those lines in the early Buddhist scriptures. Certainly, it's considered important for us to understand the *fact* of someone's anger, so that we can practice forbearance and patience:

Knowing well the other's anger, One is mindful and remains calm.

But there's little said about the need to understand others' inner lives and motivations. I guess psychotherapy was not a big thing in ancient India.

Forgiveness in early Buddhism seems to be more about knowing our *own* minds and seeing how retaliatory anger contributes to our own suffering, while also cultivating kindness:

*Happy indeed we live, friendly amidst the hostile.
Amidst hostile men we dwell free from hatred.*

Anger causes us to suffer, while forgiveness leads to peace and joy.

44. "Virtue is persecuted more by the wicked than it is loved by the good."

This particular quote is an elegant *bon mot* in a literary style that's completely foreign to the Buddhist scriptures. When I heard it I had in mind French writers of centuries past, such as Voltaire, de La Rochefoucauld, or Montaigne. However, it turned out to be straight from Cervantes' *Don Quixote*, and the words are from the Man of La Mancha himself:

I am held enchanted in this cage by the envy and fraud of wicked enchanters; for virtue is more persecuted by the wicked than loved by the good.

The irony, of course, is that in attempting to slow the spread of Fake Buddha Quotes, I'm probably tilting at windmills.

45. 'We are what we think. All that we are
    arises with our thoughts. With our thoughts
    we make the world.'

This Fake Buddha Quote, like #7 and #28,
comes to us courtesy of Thomas Byrom. It purports to be the first line of the Dhammapada.

Let's step back for a moment, get geeky, and
look at what this text actually says. In Pali it is
*Manopubbangama dhamma manosettha mano-
maya*. I'd translate this as "Experiences (*dhamma*)
are preceded by mind (*manopubbangama*), having
mind as their master (*manosettha*) created by
mind (*manomaya*)."

The only part of this translation likely to
be contentious is the word *dhamma*, which
can mean many things, including "Reality"
or "teachings." In the context of these verses,
dhamma has variously been translated as "mental states" and "mental phenomena." But I like
the word "experiences" because it's more, well,
experiential.

The overall theme of this verse (and the one
following, which starts with the same line) is how
joy and suffering arise. What the verse is saying, in context, is that any present happiness or
unhappiness we may be experiencing is the result
of what we have done with the mind in the past,

and that what we do with the mind now will affect our happiness in the future.

These verses *don't* say that we are what we think. They *don't* say that all that we are arises with our thoughts. They *don't* say that our thoughts create the world. The Buddha here is teaching psychology (how the mind works) and not ontology (the nature of reality).

Byrom was an Englishman who taught Old English, Middle English, and English literature at Oxford, and history and literature at Harvard. He was a Hindu, and he spent the last years of his life in an ashram in California. His religious affiliation may well be relevant to the way he translated these lines.

A Hindu can of course faithfully translate a Buddhist text, or a Buddhist a Hindu text, but what Byrom has done is to Hinduize the Buddha's teachings. The Hindu text the Ashtavakra Gita, which Byrom translated later in his life, does in fact say "You are what you think" (1:11), that "All creation, streaming out of the Self, is only the Self" (2:4), and that "When the world arises in me, it is just an illusion" (2:9). These concepts are not Buddhist at all, but they are what Byrom has smuggled into the Dhammapada.

While the Buddha said that we have *delusion* (*moha*) about the nature of the world, he did not say that the world was an *illusion* (*maya*). He didn't deny the existence of the external world, although he did point out that we are often mistaken about how it works. For example, he pointed out that we frequently see permanence where there is impermanence (think of every time you've fallen in and out of love), see things that cause suffering as sources of happiness (for example, we think social media will make us happy when research says the opposite is true), and believe there is a separate and permanent self when no such entity does or can exist. (These cognitive distortions, or *vipallasas*, were also mentioned when we discussed quote #3, "All worldlings are mad.")

The Buddha did not teach that we are what we think. The closest he got to this was when he said, "Whatever a monk keeps pursuing with his thinking and pondering, that becomes the inclination of his awareness." It's clear from the context, however, that he meant simply that when we repeatedly indulge in certain kinds of thought, we cultivate a habit. Again, this is a psychological teaching. If there was anything that the Buddha thought shaped us on a more profound level, it was not thought, but karma, or intentional action:

*Beings are owners of their actions (karma),
heirs of their actions; they originate from their
actions, are bound to their actions, have actions
as their refuge.*

I'm all for poetry, and Byrom's Dhammapada
is certainly poetic. It's anything but faithful to
the literal meaning of the text, however, and it's
unfortunate that it's one of the most popular
translations out there.

46. 'What you think you create, what you feel you attract, what you imagine you become.'

This quote is often attributed to the Buddha,
although it strikes me as very modern and
law-of-attraction-y. It's also found as "What you
think you become, what you feel you attract,
what you imagine you create."

I sometimes joke about "Hallmark spiritual-
ity," but in fact I believe this exact formulation to
be the words of a greeting card designer—Adele
Basheer—whose website describes this message as
her personal mantra.

Basheer has taken these phrases from the
writings of the Irish-born New Thought author

Joseph Murphy. In his 1963 book *The Power of Your Subconscious Mind* he said, "Know that belief is a thought in your mind, and what you think you create." And in his 1968 *The Cosmic Power Within You* he wrote, "You have faith when you know that thoughts are things; what you feel, you attract; and what you imagine, you become."

The Buddha's teaching doesn't have much in common with the Law of Attraction. He taught that if we want qualities like long life, beauty, happiness, status, or a good rebirth, there's no point simply wishing for them; we must do the things that lead to their arising. He certainly wouldn't agree with a statement like "all it takes is believing" (which Basheer says is also part of her personal mantra). In fact, that's a notion that he poked fun at:

> *Suppose a man were to throw a large boulder into a deep lake of water, and a great crowd of people, gathering and congregating, would pray, praise, and circumambulate with their hands palm-to-palm over the heart, saying, "Rise up, O boulder! Come floating up, O boulder! Come float to the shore, O boulder!" What do you think: would that boulder—because of the prayers, praise, and*

*circumambulation of that great crowd of peo-
ple—rise up, come floating up, or come float
to the shore?*

I can imagine that discourse raising a few
chuckles from the monks and nuns.

47. ˙Whatever is well said is a saying of the
    Blessed One.˙

This aphorism is often wheeled out like a trusty
old cannon in order to defend the habit of
misattributing quotes to the Buddha. After all,
if the Buddha himself declared that "Whatever is well said is a saying of the Blessed One"
then surely *any* decent quote can be a Buddha quote—all you have to do is stick "The
Buddha" on the end of it and it becomes auto-
matically genuine, right?

But this trusty old cannon is not what it
seems. First, it wasn't said by the Buddha. After
he hears a monk called Uttara teaching the
Dharma, Sakka, the king of the gods (*devas*)
asks if Uttara's words are his own invention or
whether he's repeating something the Buddha
had said. Uttara replies with an analogy:

Suppose that not far from a village or town there was a great pile of grain, from which a great crowd of people were carrying away grain ... If someone were to approach that great crowd of people and ask them, "From where are you carrying away grain?" answering in what way would that great crowd of people answer so as to be answering rightly?

Sakka replies:

Venerable sir, they would answer, "We are carrying it from that great pile of grain," so as to be answering rightly.

To which Uttara responds:

In the same way, deva-king, whatever is well said is all a saying of the Blessed One, the Worthy One, the Rightly Self-awakened One. Adopting it again and again from there do we and others speak.

Second, in context we can see that this quote doesn't mean what you probably thought it did at first glance. Uttara is saying that he's been to the grain pile of the Buddha's words, and has offered that grain to Sakka. He seems to be saying "whatever I have said *that is well said* is the word of the Buddha."

This is not unlike a sentiment often found in book acknowledgments, along the lines of, "Whatever is of value here comes from my teachers; the errors are all my own." Uttara was not saying that if Madame de Staël, Robert Louis Stevenson, or Marie Curie came up with a neat turn of phrase, that it was actually a quote from the Buddha.

48. 'When the student is ready the teacher will appear.'

This quote is all over the internet, and in several books, both as a "Buddhist proverb" and directly attributed to the Buddha. It's originally from an 1885 book called *Light on the Path*, by the theosophist Mabel Collins (see also #34). In Collins's book the quote is in the form, "For when the disciple is ready the Master is ready also." Collins doesn't attribute it to the Buddha.

Theosophy is a spiritual movement, cofounded by Madame Helena Blavatsky and Colonel Henry Olcott, aiming to synthesize Eastern religious traditions with Western esoteric teachings. It made some unusual claims to authenticity. For example, the title page of *Light on the Path* says that the book was "written down" by Collins. Why this odd form of words? Well, the Theosophists claimed to be in psychic contact with "Masters" in the East who dictated works to them, and so Collins presented herself not as an author, but as Stenographer to the Enlightened. Later in her life, however, she expressed regret at having fraudulently claimed that the book was dictated to her in this way.

Theosophists were in fact widely accused of plagiarism and of counterfeiting teachings. In 1884 Richard Hodgson of the British Society for Psychical Research called Blavatsky "one of the most accomplished, ingenious and interesting impostors in history." In an 1895 article, William Emmette Coleman claimed that there were 2,000 instances of plagiarism in Blavatsky's signature work, *Isis Unveiled*. He pointed out that another of her works, *Voice of the Silence*, which Blavatsky claimed was a translation of a Tibetan teaching, was in fact "a compilation of ideas and terminology from various nineteenth-century books."

Fake Buddha Quotes are one thing, but Blavatsky took this to new levels by faking an entire sutra! Although Mabel Collins recanted, Blavatsky, a consummate con artist, maintained her cover story to the bitter end.

49. ˙Without health life is not life; it is only a state of languor and suffering—an image of death.˙

This saying is attributed to the Buddha on many quotes sites, in several books, and (at a rough guess) in a gazillion health-related blogs or articles. You can even buy it on a coffee mug.

This quote struck me as bogus because the Buddha taught us to live at peace with the reality of illness, old age and death. For example, in talking with a sick and aged householder, he said:

The body is afflicted, weak, and encumbered. For who, looking after this body, would claim even a moment of true health, except through sheer foolishness? So you should train yourself: "Even though I may be afflicted in body, my mind will be unafflicted."

When we bear in mind the reality of impermanence, a healthy body is just a sick body waiting to happen. This might sound depressing, but depression in the face of sickness was precisely what the Buddha was counseling against; depression arises from the expectation that illness won't, or shouldn't, happen. By recognizing that we can't ultimately control the destiny of this body, on the other hand, we can observe our illness in a detached and serene way rather than being brought down by it.

The quote in question is actually from the French Renaissance writer François Rabelais, and is found in the prologue to the fourth book of his magnum opus, *Gargantua and Pantagruel*.

I wonder how many people have the mug?

50. "Your work is to discover your work and then with all your heart give yourself to it."

Our final Fake Buddha Quote is one of the most popular. It's found also in the form: "Your work is to discover your *world* and then with all your heart give yourself to it." Neither version sounded even vaguely genuine to me, and both turned out to be adapted from Anne Bancroft's rendering of the Dhammapada, where her rendition of verse 166 says:

*Your work is to find out what your work should
be and not to neglect it for another's. Clearly
discover your work and attend to it with all
your heart.*

Incidentally, this Anne Bancroft is not the
American actress famous for playing the role of
Mrs. Robinson in *The Graduate*, but a British
Buddhist and author. The two women were
sometimes confused for each other. The Buddhist Bancroft once turned up to give a talk
and found herself surrounded by paparazzi
expecting the American actress, and one of her
articles on Zen Buddhism was illustrated with
very un-Zen-like pictures of her actress name-
sake with cigarette in hand. Bancroft is also the
mother of Deb Shapiro, whom we met in our
discussion of quote #38.

In Narada Thera's translation of the Dhammapada, verse 166 says:

*For the sake of others' welfare, however great,
let not one neglect one's own welfare. Clearly
perceiving one's own welfare, let one be intent
on one's own goal.*

Gil Fronsdal's version is:

Don't give up your own welfare
For the sake of others' welfare, however great.
Clearly know your own welfare,
And be intent on the highest good.

Both of these translations are fairly literal, while Bancroft's rendition is little more than a wild paraphrase. The word translated by Narada and Fronsdal as "welfare" is *attha*, which means interest, advantage, gain, profit, or even purpose. It's usually understood along the lines of "spiritual welfare." It has nothing directly to do with work, and it's a puzzle why Bancroft thought it was.

Just as Byrom's Dhammapada is described as a "rendering," Bancroft is credited not as "translator" of her version but as "editor." What both Bancroft and Byrom seem to have done (and Bancroft more or less admits this in the introduction to her Dhammapada) was to work from existing translations, sometimes consulting a Pali–English dictionary. The trouble is that without a working knowledge of the grammar of the language you're translating, you're essentially left blindly guessing what the original means. I call this approach the pin-the-meaning-on-the-scripture style of translation.

There can of course be great latitude in how a particular text is translated, and there are many valid reasons why two translations of the same passage look very different. But often the texts are quite clear, as this particular passage is.

Incidentally, the original, with its emphasis on not sacrificing your welfare for the sake of others, is certainly not suggesting that we shouldn't help other people if it inconveniences us, although you'd be forgiven for thinking that. (The Buddha once personally took care of a monk who had dysentery and encouraged the practice of compassion.)

Bancroft's rendition would lead most people to think that the verse is about the kind of employment you choose. But it's not.

This verse is actually about not getting sidetracked from our spiritual practice by devotion to teachers. Each Dhammapada verse has attached to it an anecdote that helps us understand its message and explains the circumstances in which it was originally taught. The commentary to this particular verse tells the tale of a monk who didn't go to visit the Buddha while the latter was on his deathbed, because he was determined to become fully awakened. Although the monk was criticized for seemingly not showing sufficient love and devotion, the Buddha was perfectly happy that his disciple had chosen to pay homage to him by striving for the goal of awakening.

Bancroft's version is lovely and inspiring. Yes, we should no doubt discover a vocation and give ourselves to it fully. But that's not what the Buddha was encouraging us to do in this verse; he was asking us to go all the way to awakening.

CONCLUSION

. . . .

Quote-Checking as a
Spiritual Practice

It's wonderful that people are moved to share
inspiring and thought-provoking quotes, and
I celebrate that generosity of spirit. I love how
we yearn to encounter words of wisdom. I love
how we resonate with them. I love how we
instinctively recognize we're in the presence of
a perspective truer and deeper than our normal
way of seeing things, and expressed more ele-
gantly than the mundane communication to
which we're usually exposed.

I also love the Buddha's teaching. Because of this love I'd like to see us represent him and other teachers in their own terms, and not impose a distorted lens of misinformation between them and us. Some of the quotes we've seen are benign paraphrases, but others present the Buddha as an exponent of rationalism, or Hinduism, or the Law or Attraction or other forms of New Thought. Even sincerely practicing Buddhists can have difficulty disentangling these non-Buddhist perspectives from the Dharma the Buddha actually taught.

I encourage all Buddhist practitioners to spend time imbibing the scriptures. Most of us get started by reading books written by modern teachers such as Sharon Salzberg, Jack Kornfield, Pema Chödrön, Lama Surya Das, and so on. These writers present Buddhist practice in accessible language and on the basis of considerable personal experience. They are wise and insightful teachers. But if we don't get a feel for the content and style of the original scriptures, we're vulnerable to being taken in by fake quotes.

I'm perplexed when people write and tell me that accurate attributions and translations aren't important, and that the only things that matter are whether quotes are true and how they make us feel. They and I evidently see these things in very different ways. I agree that the truth of a statement doesn't depend on whose name is at the end of it. Neither, in essence, does its ability to inspire.* However, the attribution that's attached to a quote does matter. It is a statement of fact: such-and-such a person said this. When a quote we share is misattributed or distorted, we're passing on information that's false.

To unknowingly pass on a quote that's misattributed or inaccurate is one thing. We're all fallible. But not to care about doing this is another matter. Surely it should be uncontroversial that it's better to share truth rather than falsehood? Also, I value fairness: I'd like to see us credit the true authors of quotes, rather than misattribute their work and deny them their due as creators.

Just as most of us have inadvertently passed on to our online friends misattributed or distorted quotes, many of us have unwittingly passed on fake news stories. I don't think it's a stretch to see these two phenomena as connected.

There are people who invent stories for reasons of political partisanship, or to make money

---

* However, as Ethel Fischbaum noted, "One reason so many quotations are misattributed is that words are taken more seriously when attached to the name of a famous person."

by driving traffic to their websites, or simply for the enjoyment they get from manipulating others. These articles are often designed to provoke us emotionally, which has the side-effect of making us less rational and more uncritical. Before we know it, we've been conned into sharing a false narrative that "shows" how stupid, intolerant, or evil our political opponents are. Our minds become weaponized by the hateful, the greedy, and the mischievous.

When our minds are hijacked in this way, we inadvertently allow ourselves to be used as tools to damage something I think we all, deep down, love. I believe that beneath our outrage is a desire to relate to each other with mutual respect, to find ways to disagree civilly, and to recognize our common humanity. But our sharing of untruth pushes us into separate social bubbles, as people who have different values from us "unfriend" us, or as we do the same to them.

These days I find myself checking just about any quote before I pass it on, especially where the content is political. For example, the majority of quotes I've seen on social media that purport to be from the Founding Fathers of the United States—whether being put forward to support a liberal or conservative agenda—are either invented or taken out of context. I also see many images of contemporary political figures to which have been added manufactured quotations or distorted narratives that show them in a bad light.

So I encourage the following practice: pause before you share. I encourage us all to take a moment before passing on a quote or a news story in order to do a little research. Someone (and I'm pretty sure it wasn't the Buddha) said that "Google before you share" is the new "think before you speak."

Taking a moment to fact-check stories and quotes is good for us on a spiritual level. One of the distinctive features of the Buddha's teaching is an emphasis on being mindful of our feelings, and of learning not to react to them with attachment or aversion. Provocative "news" stories are designed to inflame our emotions and make us act without thinking. Do we really want to be manipulated in this way, or would we rather act in a way that's mindful and self-possessed?

Training yourself to be mindful of your feelings teaches you how to avoid being exploited. Taking a sacred pause when your emotional buttons have been pressed is a way of reclaiming your own mind and your autonomy as a human being. This also applies to sharing what inspires us; as the desire to share a quote that moves us builds, we can pause and let our desire for truth-fulness catch up with our enthusiasm.

Checking our sources helps check our emotions. When we research with the genuine intention to seek the truth, we engage our neocortex. This is the part of the brain where higher reasoning takes place and where self-control originates. It's the most distinctively human part of our brains, and so by training ourselves to respond to the world with thoughtfulness, curiosity, and a little skepticism, rather than reacting emotionally, we literally become more human.

Fact-checking gives us an opportunity to practice our critical thinking skills. We can learn which sources are likely to be trustworthy and not believe the first thing we see online ("It must be true; I saw it on the internet!") and avoid practicing confirmation bias by looking only for information that reinforces what we want to believe. (Pro tip: quotes sites exist to make money, and fake quotes attract as many eyeballs and advertising dollars as genuine ones do.) We can learn that just because something is repeated by many people, it's not necessarily true. In the case of fake news, we can learn to look for signs that someone is trying to manipulate us.

In his quest to discover a true perspective on life, the Buddha abandoned all that was dear to him and spent years scrutinizing his experience to see what it could teach him about the nature of Reality. Eventually he attained awakening, and saw things as they really are. If we're inspired by his words, then perhaps we'll choose to be inspired by his life too, and likewise work to seek, love, and protect the truth.

Taking responsibility for what we share is an opportunity to show care and respect for the culture around us and all beings affected by it. Hopefully by doing these things we can make the world a better place.

When we consider the vast complexity of the societies in which we live, we may think that our individual actions can have little effect. But we should never underestimate our power to create change. "It takes just one snowball to start an avalanche," as the Buddha never said.

TWENTY-FIVE QUOTABLE
(AND REAL) QUOTES

1. "You yourself must strive. The Buddhas only point the way."

2. "If you do not grasp at anything in the present you will go about at peace."

3. "Ardently do today what must be done. Who knows? Tomorrow, death comes."

4. "Whatever is not yours: let go of it. Your letting go of it will be for your long-term happiness and benefit."

5. "I am the owner of my actions, heir to my actions, born of my actions, related through my actions, and have my actions as my arbitrator. Whatever I do, for good or for evil, to that will I fall heir."

6. "Some do not understand that we must die, but those who do realize this settle their quarrels."

7. "Ceasing to do evil, cultivating the good, purifying the heart: This is the teaching of the Buddhas."

8. "Should you find a wise critic to point out your faults, follow him as you would a guide to hidden treasure."

9. "If with a pure mind a person speaks or acts, happiness follows them like a never-departing shadow."

10. "Drop by drop is the water pot filled. Likewise, the wise man, gathering it little by little, fills himself with good."

11. "Give, even if you only have a little."

12. "It is in the nature of things that joy arises in a person free from remorse."

13. "Meditate ... do not delay, lest you later regret it."

14. "A disciplined mind brings happiness."

15. "Rouse yourself! Sit up! Resolutely train yourself to attain peace."

16. "Looking after oneself, one looks after others. Looking after others, one looks after oneself."

17. *"As I am, so are these. As are these, so am I.* Drawing the parallel to yourself, neither kill nor get others to kill."

18. "Just as with her own life, a mother shields from hurt her own son, her only child, let all-embracing thoughts for all beings be yours."

19. "We will develop and cultivate the liberation of mind by kindness, make it our vehicle, make it our basis, stabilize it, exercise ourselves in it, and fully perfect it."

20. "Conquer anger with non-anger. Conquer badness with goodness. Conquer meanness with generosity. Conquer dishonesty with truth."

21. "Whatever has the nature of arising has the nature of ceasing."

22. "The wise do not grieve, having realized the nature of the world."

23. "There is no fear for one whose mind is not filled with desires."

24. "Not as higher, lower, nor equal do they refer to themselves. With birth ended, the holy life fulfilled, they go about, totally freed from fetters."

25. "Just as the great ocean has one taste, the taste of salt, so also this Dhamma and Discipline has one taste, the taste of liberation."

WHERE TO FIND THE REAL DEAL

Websites

Throughout this book I've referred to online resources as much as possible, rather than printed books, so that you, the reader, can more easily check out the original scriptures. Most of the references are to the website Access to Insight (accesstoinsight.org), which hosts a wide variety of the Pali scriptures. I highly recommend this as a place to start exploring the Buddha's teaching.

I also recommend Sutta Central (suttacentral.net), a more recent and, at the time of publication, still-evolving site, which is currently less easy to use but offers a greater variety of texts and translations.

Books

The Dhammapada, which I've often cited in this book, is an excellent place to start exploring the Buddha's teaching. Of the many translations available, I consider Gil Fronsdal's excellent at being poetic and yet remaining faithful to the original text.*

Bhikkhu Bodhi is a superhero of modern translation. (I just found myself googling "Bhikkhu Bodhi action figure"—sadly without result.) His book, *In the Buddha's Words*, provides an anthology of scriptural passages, arranged by theme. The selections are prefaced by essays that in themselves provide an excellent introduction to the Buddha's thought. The publisher of that book (Wisdom Publications) offers other collections of Buddhist texts. These include *The Middle Length Discourses of the Buddha*, *The Connected Discourses of the Buddha*, *The Numerical Discourses*

---

* Gil Fronsdal, trans., *The Dhammapada: A New Translation of the Buddhist Classic with Annotations* (Boston: Shambhala, 2006).

of the Buddha, and *The Suttanipata*, which are all translated by Bhikkhu Bodhi, and *The Long Discourses of the Buddha*, translated by Maurice Walshe. These titles are an excellent resource for the serious student.

Resources for Studying Pali

I spent two years studying Pali at university—which taught me about enough to be able to order a cup of coffee, translate some of the simpler discourses, or tell a householder that his goat has been eaten by jackals. In other words I'm no expert. But if you have the interest I'd highly recommend learning a little of the language.

A Pali-English dictionary will help you a little, but it's very handy to know some of the grammar so that you can tell how words are related to each other. Like Latin, Pali is a language where the ending of a noun tells you whether that noun is doing something to you, you are doing something to it, whether you belong to the noun, are inside it, and so forth. Without grammatical context you're, as I say, trying to pin the meaning on the tail of the scripture.

There are many resources available online or as books, but I'd recommend starting with Dr. Lily de Silva's *Pali Primer* (Vipassana

Research Publications, 1994) which introduces the grammar and vocabulary in the context of fun sentences that start very simple and gradually become more complex. It won't get you translating suttas, but it'll give you a flying start when you graduate to a more hard-core program of study.

NOTES

• •

Introduction

9   *"I can't. This is important"*: Randall Munroe,
"Duty Calls" XKCD, accessed 24 Nov, 2017
https://xkcd.com/386/.

11   *"the Cetana sutta"*: Thanissaro Bhikkhu (Tr.),
"Cetana Sutta: An Act of Will" (AN 11.2), Access
to Insight (BCBS Edition), 4 July 2010, http://
www.accesstoinsight.org/tipitaka/an/an11/
an11.002.than.html.

11   *"simply another form of mental illness"*: Lama Yeshe,

The Peaceful Stillness of the Silent Mind (Lincoln, MA: Lama Yeshe Wisdom Archive, 2004), 49.

12 *"there is no grief, whence then fear?"*: Acharya Buddharakkhita, "Piyavagga: Affection," Access to Insight (BCBS Edition), 30 November 2013, http://www.accesstoinsight.org/tipitaka/kn/dhp/dhp.16.budd.html.

15 *"set their hearts on knowing them"*: Thanissaro Bhikkhu, "Ani Sutta: The Peg," Access to Insight (BCBS Edition), 30 November 2013, http://www.accesstoinsight.org/tipitaka/sn/sn20/sn20.007.than.html.

16 *"pardon each other's folly"*: François Voltaire, *Philosophical Dictionary* (London: George Allen & Unwin, 1923), 302.

The Quotes

18 *"not the purpose of being clung to"*: Nyanaponika Thera, "Alagaddupama Sutta: The Snake Simile," Access to Insight (BCBS Edition), 30 November 2013, http://www.accesstoinsight.org/tipitaka/mn/mn.022.nypo.html.

20 *"not to get what one wants is suffering"*: Ñanamoli Thera "Dhammacakkappavattana Sutta: Setting the Wheel of Dhamma in Motion," Access to

Insight (BCBS Edition), 13 June 2010, http://
www.accesstoinsight.org/tipitaka/sn/sn56/
sn56.011.nymo.html.

22 *"The worldling is like a madman"*: *"Ummattako
viya hi puthujjano."* Bhikkhu Ñanamoli, *Visuddhimagga: The Path of Purification* (Colombo:
Buddhist Publication Society, 2010), 595.

23 *"things that are wholesome are unwholesome"*:
Andrew Olendzki, "Vipallasa Sutta: Distortions
of the Mind," Access to Insight (BCBS Edition), 2
November 2013, http://www.accesstoinsight.org/
tipitaka/an/an04/an04.049.olen.html.

24 *"his desire and pride increase"*: Acharya Buddharakkhita, "Balavagga: The Fool," Access
to Insight (BCBS Edition), 30 November
2013, http://www.accesstoinsight.org/tipitaka/kn/
dhp/dhp.05.budd.html.

24 *"one protects one's store of wealth"*: Thanissaro
Bhikkhu, "Dighajanu (Vyagghapajja) Sutta: To
Dighajanu," Access to Insight (BCBS Edition), 30
November 2013, http://www.accesstoinsight.org/
tipitaka/an/an08/an08.054.than.html.

25 *"the blessings of the holy life"*: Acharya Buddharakkhita, "Yamakavagga: Pairs," Access to Insight
(BCBS Edition), 30 November 2013, http://
www.accesstoinsight.org/tipitaka/kn/dhp/dhp.01.
budd.html.

27 *"so I preach to all"*: W. E. Soothill, *The Lotus of*

the *Wonderful Law* (Oxford: Clarendon Press, 1922), 127.

28 *"is called just"*: Dhammapada 257: Acharya Buddharakkhita, "Dhammatthavagga: The Just," Access to Insight (BCBS Edition), 30 November 2013, http://www.accesstoinsight.org/tipitaka/kn/dhp/dhp.19.budd.html.

32 *"enter and remain in them"*: Thanissaro Bhikkhu, "Kalama Sutta: To the Kalamas," Access to Insight (BCBS Edition), 30 November 2013, http://www.accesstoinsight.org/tipitaka/an/an03/an03.065.than.html.

36 *"drowsiness once it has arisen"*: Thanissaro Bhikkhu, "Ahara Sutta: Food," Access to Insight (BCBS Edition), 30 November 2013, http://www.accesstoinsight.org/tipitaka/sn/sn46/sn46.051.than.html.

38 *"Karma, I tell you, is intention"*: Thanissaro Bhikkhu, "Nibbedhika Sutta: Penetrative," Access to Insight (BCBS Edition), 30 November 2013, http://www.accesstoinsight.org/tipitaka/an/an06/an06.063.than.html.

38 *"the welfare of all living beings"*: Ñanamoli Thera, "Cula-kammavibhanga Sutta: The Shorter Exposition of Kamma," Access to Insight (BCBS Edition), 30 November 2013, http://www.accesstoinsight.org/tipitaka/mn/mn.135.nymo.html.

39   *"what was done in the past"*: Thanissaro Bhik-
     khu "Tittha Sutta: Sectarians," Access to Insight
     (BCBS Edition), 30 November 2013, http://www.
     accesstoinsight.org/tipitaka/an/an03/an03.061.
     than.html.

40   *"subject to cessation"*: See for example, Thanissaro
     Bhikkhu, "Upatissa-pasine: Upatissa's (Sariputta's)
     Question," Access to Insight (BCBS Edition), 30
     November 2013, http://www.accesstoinsight.org/
     tipitaka/vin/mv/mv.01.23.01-10.than.html.

40   *"published in 1994"*: Jack Kornfield, *Buddha's Little
     Instruction Book* (New York: Bantam, 1994), 68.

41   *"spoken by the Tathagata"*: Thanissaro Bhikkhu
     "Abhasita Sutta: What Was Not Said," Access to
     Insight (Legacy Edition), 4 August 2010, http://
     www.accesstoinsight.org/tipitaka/an/an02/
     an02.023.than.html.

43   *"what you think about it"*: Dale Carnegie, *How
     to Win Friends and Influence People* (New York:
     Pocket Books, 1998), 67.

43   *"never-departing shadow"*: Acharya Buddharak-
     khita, "Yamakavagga: Pairs," Access to Insight
     (BCBS Edition), 30 November 2013, http://
     www.accesstoinsight.org/tipitaka/kn/dhp/dhp.01.
     budd.html.

45   *"wish for another to suffer"*: Thanissaro Bhikkhu,
     "The Khuddakapatha," Access to Insight (BCBS

Edition), 30 November 2013, http://www.access-toinsight.org/tipitaka/kn/khp/khp.1-9.than.html.

46   *"the benefit of the poison"*: Emmet Fox, *The Sermon on the Mount* (New York: HarperCollins, 1989), 91.

48   *"it would be very discouraging"*: Eve Curie, *Madame Curie: A Biography* (Garden City, New York: Doubleday, 1937), 116.

49   *"who we are and what the world is"*: Jorge Luis Borges, *Jorge Luis Borges: A Personal Anthology* (New York: Grove Press, 1967), 136.

49   *"what God and man is"*: Edmund Clarence Stedman, *A Victorian Anthology, 1837-1895* (Cambridge, Mass.: Riverside Press, 1896), 211.

50   *"within this fathom-long body"*: See, for example, Thanissaro Bhikkhu "Rohitassa Sutta: To Rohitassa," Access to Insight (BCBS Edition), 30 November 2013, http://www.accesstoinsight.org/tipitaka/an/an04/an04.045.than.html.

50   *"see a specialist"*: David M. Bader, *Zen Judaism: For You a Little Enlightenment* (New York: Harmony Books, 2007), 25.

51   *"mind of loving-kindness"*: Bhikkhu Bodhi, *The Numerical Discourses of the Buddha* (Boston, MA: Wisdom, 2012), 816.

52   *"the shit that weighs you down"*: Toni Morrison, *Song of Solomon* (New York, NY: Vintage International, 2004), 179.

53   *"they are dear to themselves"*: Thanissaro Bhik-
     khu "Piya Sutta: Dear," Access to Insight (BCBS
     Edition), 30 November 2013, http://www.access-
     toinsight.org/tipitaka/sn/sn03/sn03.004.than.html.

55   *"lamentation, longing, and sorrow"*: Thanissaro
     Bhikkhu "Salla Sutta: The Arrow," Access to
     Insight (BCBS Edition), 30 November 2013,
     http://www.accesstoinsight.org/tipitaka/kn/snp/
     snp.3.08.than.html.

57   *"fills himself with good"*: Acharya Buddharakkh-
     ita, "Papavagga: Evil," Access to Insight (BCBS
     Edition), 30 November 2013, http://www.acces-
     stoinsight.org/tipitaka/kn/dhp/dhp.09.budd.html.

57   *"that can prevail"*: Arthur Waley, *Tao Te Ching*
     (Ware, Herts.: Wordsworth Editions, 1997), 82.

58   *"does not come to an end"*: Bhikkhuni Uppa-
     lavanna, "Pabbata Sutta," *Wikipitaka: The
     Completing Tipitaka,* accessed Oct 15, 2017, http://
     tipitaka.wikia.com/wiki/Pabbata_Sutta.

59   *"the absence of distinctions"*: "Writings of Nichiren
     Daishonin, Volume II," *Soka Gakkai Nichiren
     Buddhism Library,* accessed Oct 16, 2017, http://
     www.nichirenlibrary.org/en/wnd-2/Con-
     tent/315#para-68.

61   *"In that way, monks, you should reject it"*: Sister
     Vajira and Francis Story, "Maha-parinibbana
     Sutta: Last Days of the Buddha," Access
     to Insight (BCBS Edition), 30 November

2013, http://www.accesstoinsight.org/tipitaka/dn/dn.16.1-6.vaji.html.

62 *"true success is to labor"*: Robert Louis Stevenson, *Virginibus Puerisque* (New York: Charles Scribner's Sons, 1910), 170.

63 *"the only moment we have"*: Thich Nhat Hanh, *No Death, No Fear* (New York: Riverhead Books, 2002), 100.

63 *"Elsewhere"*: Thich Nhat Hanh, *Cultivating the Mind of Love*, (Berkeley, CA: Parallax Press, 1998), 81

64 *"has not been reached"*: Bhikkhu Bodhi, *The Middle Length Discourses of the Buddha* (Boston: Wisdom Publications, 1995), 1039.

65 *"a kindness done"*: Thanissaro Bhikkhu, "Dullabha Sutta: Hard to Find," Access to Insight (BCBS Edition), 4 August 2010, http://www.accesstoinsight.org/tipitaka/an/an02/an02.119.than.html.

65 *"one of my followers"*: Translation simplified from Bhikkhu Bodhi, *Connected Discourses of the Buddha* (Boston, MA: Wisdom, 2000). 712.

66 *"other than Freedom"*: Thomas Carlyle, *Sartor Resartus* (Oxford: Oxford University Press, 1987), 140.

67 *"not broken through to"*: Thanissaro Bhikkhu, "Kotthita Sutta: With Kotthita," Access to Insight (BCBS Edition), 30 November 2013, http://www.accesstoinsight.org/tipitaka/an/an09/an09.013.than.html.

68 *"a holy man"*: Acharya Buddharakkhita, "Brahmanavagga: The Holy Man," Access to Insight (BCBS Edition), 30 November 2013, http://www.accesstoinsight.org/tipitaka/kn/dhp/dhp.26.budd.html.

68 *"the moon freed from clouds"*: Acharya Buddharakkhita, "Bhikkhuvagga: The Monk," Access to Insight (BCBS Edition), 30 November 2013, http://www.accesstoinsight.org/tipitaka/kn/dhp/dhp.25.budd.html.

70 *"I have not given you a system"*: Osho, "The Diamond Sutra: The Buddha Also Said," (London: Watkins Media, 2017).

72 *"bound up with suffering"*: John D. Ireland, "Salla Sutta: The Arrow," Access to Insight (BCBS Edition), 30 November 2013, http://www.accesstoinsight.org/tipitaka/kn/snp/snp.3.08.irel.html.

72 *"keep on seeking outside"*: Ruth Fuller Sasaki, *The Record of Linji* (Honolulu: University of Hawai'i Press, 2009), 22.

74 *"disagreeable to me"*: Bhikkhu Bodhi, *The Connected Discourses of the Buddha* (Boston, MA: Wisdom, 2000), 1797.

76 *"in order to develop insight"*: See for example, Thanissaro Bhikkhu "Kimattha Sutta: What is the Purpose?" Access to Insight (BCBS Edition), 30 November 2013, http://www.accesstoinsight.org/tipitaka/an/an11/an11.001.than.html.

77 *"you wanted to suffer"*: Osho, "Voice of Silence," Osho.com, http://www.osho.com/iosho/library/read-book/online-library-hillary-tensing-suffering-e0b5ed43-3a5?p=9641afa86abbc0d-742d19532ad0847bd

77 *"as though joined with it"*: Thanissaro Bhikkhu, "Sallatha Sutta: The Arrow," Access to Insight (BCBS Edition), 30 November 2013, http://www.accesstoinsight.org/tipitaka/sn/sn36/sn36.006.than.html.

78 *"like an enemy"*: Kate Crosby and Andrew Skilton, *The Bodhicaryavatara* (Oxford: Oxford World's Classics, 1995), 7.

79 *"by the wise for themselves"*: For example, see Thanissaro Bhikkhu, "Gilana Sutta: Sick" Access to Insight (BCBS Edition), 30 November 2013, http://www.accesstoinsight.org/tipitaka/sn/sn41/sn41.010.than.html. "To be realized by the wise for themselves" is *veditabbo viññuhi*.

79 *"to be experienced by the wise"*: For example, see Thanissaro Bhikkhu, "Aggi-Vacchagotta Sutta: To Vacchagotta on Fire," Access to Insight (BCBS Edition), 30 November 2013, http://www.accesstoinsight.org/tipitaka/mn/mn.072.than.html. "To be experienced by the wise" is *panditavedaniyo*.

80 *"charming, profitable, and easeful"*: Thanissaro Bhikkhu, "Bija Sutta: The Seed" Access to Insight

(BCBS Edition), 30 November 2013, http://www.
accesstoinsight.org/tipitaka/an/an10/an10.104.
than.html.

85 *"deep in the forest"*: Thanissaro Bhikkhu,
"Nagara Sutta: The City," Access to Insight
(BCBS Edition), 30 November 2013, http://
www.accesstoinsight.org/tipitaka/sn/sn12/
sn12.065.than.html.

86 *"failure, not success"*: Thanissaro Bhikkhu,
"Micchatta Sutta: Wrongness," Access to Insight
(BCBS Edition), 30 November 2013, http://www.
accesstoinsight.org/tipitaka/an/an10/an10.103.
than.html.

87 *"peace of mind"*: Bhikkhu Bodhi, *The Numerical
Discourses of the Buddha* (Boston: Wisdom Publications, 2012), 233.

91 *"to the profit of both"*: Maurice O'Connell Walshe,
"Sangaravo Sutta: Sangarava," Access to Insight
(BCBS Edition), 30 November 2013, http://www.
accesstoinsight.org/tipitaka/sn/sn46/sn46.055.
wlsh.html.

93 *"still their hatred"*: Acharya Buddharakkhita,
"Yamakavagga: Pairs," Access to Insight (BCBS
Edition), 30 November 2013, http://www.access-
toinsight.org/tipitaka/kn/dhp/dhp.01.budd.html.

94 *"confessed his transgression"*: Thanissaro Bhikkhu,
"Bala-pandita Sutta: Fools & Wise People," Access
to Insight (BCBS Edition), 4 August 2010, http://

www.accesstoinsight.org/tipitaka/an/an02/
an02.021.than.html.

94   *"mindful and remains calm"*: Andrew Olendzki,
     "Vepacitti Sutta: Calm in the Face of Anger,"
     Access to Insight (BCBS Edition), 2 November
     2013, http://www.accesstoinsight.org/tipitaka/sn/
     sn11/sn11.004.olen.html.

95   *"free from hatred"*: Acharya Buddharakkhita,
     "Sukhavagga: Happiness," Access to Insight
     (BCBS Edition), 30 November 2013, http://
     www.accesstoinsight.org/tipitaka/kn/dhp/dhp.15.
     budd.html

95   *"loved by the good"*: Miguel de Cervantes, *The
     Ingenious Gentleman Don Quixote of La Man-
     cha, Volume 2*, (London: Smith, Elder, & Co.,
     1885), 327.

97   *"translated later in his life"*: Thomas Byrom, *The
     Heart of Awareness: A Translation of the Ashta-
     vakra Gita* (Boston: Shambhala, 1990). Byrom's
     rendition of the Dhammapada is still in print:
     Dhammapada: The Sayings of the Buddha (Boston:
     Shambhala, 1976).

99   *"actions as their refuge"*: Bhikkhu Bodhi, *The
     Middle Length Discourses of the Buddha* (Boston:
     Wisdom Publications, 1995), 1053.

100 *"lead to their arising"*: See for example Thanissaro
     Bhikkhu, "Ittha Sutta: What is Welcome," Access
     to Insight (BCBS Edition), 30 November

2013, http://www.accesstoinsight.org/tipitaka/an/an05/an05.043.than.html.

101 *"float to the shore?"*: Thanissaro Bhikkhu, "Paccha-bhumika Sutta: [Brahmans] of the Western Land" (SN 42.6)". Access to Insight (BCBS Edition), 30 November 2013, http://www.accesstoinsight.org/tipitaka/sn/sn42/sn42.006.than.html

102 *"we and others speak"*: Thanissaro Bhikkhu "Uttara Sutta: About Uttara," Access to Insight (BCBS Edition), 30 November 2013, http://www.accesstoinsight.org/tipitaka/an/an08/an08.008.than.html.

104 *"Isis Unveiled"*: Vsevolod Sergyeevich Solovyoff, *A Modern Priestess of Isis* (London: Longmans, Green, and Co., 1895), 353–366.

105 *"my mind will be unafflicted"*: Thanissaro Bhikkhu, "Nakulapita Sutta: To Nakulapita," *Access to Insight* (BCBS Edition), 30 November 2013, http://www.accesstoinsight.org/tipitaka/sn/sn22/sn22.001.than.html.

107 *"intent on one's own goal"*: Narada Thera, *The Dhammapada* 4th Edition, (Taipei, Taiwan: The Corporate Body of the Buddha Educational Foundation, 1993), 150.

108 *"intent on the highest good"*: Gil Fronsdal, *The Dhammapada: Teachings of the Buddha* (Boston: Shambhala, 2005), 41.

ACKNOWLEDGMENTS

• •

My exploration of Fake Buddha Quotes has been aided and abetted by many people over the years. A Buddhist friend, Jnanagarbha (aka Alan Ashley) was the first person to discuss with me the phenomenon of misattributed quotes on Twitter, and the fun we had together was what first led to me documenting them on my personal blog. Thanks, brother!

Unfortunately I can no longer recall (and haven't been able to track down) the name of the person who first suggested that I create a dedicated blog to the topic. I'm grateful for the encouragement.

Many people over the years have submitted quotes for verification or debunking. Thank you! Several researchers have come to my aid with information about quotes, most notably renowned etymologist Barry Popik, who tracked down the source of "When the student is ready the teacher will appear," and Garson O'Toole of the Quote Investigator website, who found the author of the quote that begins "Resolve to be tender with the young."

My editor at Tricycle, Emma Varvaloucas, was the first to approach me to publish a number of Fake Buddha Quote columns at that magazine. Rod Meade Sperry of *Lion's Roar* magazine asked me to write a similar article in that publication. Thank you, Emma and Rod. The *Lion's Roar* piece is what caught the attention of the fine folks at Parallax, which brings me to express my gratitude to my editor there, Jacob Surpin, who has been a delight to work with.

Lastly, I'm deeply indebted to, and in awe of, the many people who have expended so much effort and put so much love into translating the Buddhist scriptures and making them available to the modern world. Three contemporary translators stand out for me: Bhikkhu Bodhi,

Thanissaro Bhikkhu, and Bhikkhu Sujato. These three men are, to me, Dharma Superheroes, and I hereby dub them "The League of Extraordinary Gentle-Bhikkhus."

RELATED TITLES

Awakening of the Heart
Thich Nhat Hanh

Biography of Silence
Pablo d'Ors

The Dhammapada
Ananda Maitreya

How to Sit
Thich Nhat Hanh

Old Path White Clouds
Thich Nhat Hanh

The Other Shore
Thich Nhat Hanh

 **PARALLAX PRESS**

Parallax Press, a nonprofit publisher founded
by Zen Master Thich Nhat Hanh, publishes
books and media on the art of mindful living
and Engaged Buddhism. We are committed to
offering teachings that help transform suffering
and injustice. Our aspiration is to contribute to
collective insight and awakening, bringing about
a more joyful, healthy, and compassionate society.

For a copy of the catalog, please contact:

Parallax Press
P.O. Box 7355
Berkeley, CA 94707
parallax.org